BOOKS BY THE AUTHOR

Window Sill Gardening

Greenhouse Gardening As A Hobby

The New World Encyclopedia of Outdoor Gardening

Foliage Plants for Indoor Gardening

FOLIAGE PLANTS FOR
INDOOR GARDENING

FOLIAGE PLANTS

for

INDOOR GARDENING

by James Underwood Crockett

COLOR PHOTOGRAPHS BY THE AUTHOR

BLACK AND WHITE PHOTOGRAPHS BY ROCHE

Doubleday & Company, Inc., Garden City, N.Y.

To the florists of America,
many of whom have been my friends since childhood,
all of whom share with me a love for living plants,
and who, in their daily work,
bring beauty into the lives of others.

CONTENTS

Contents

Contents

LIST OF ILLUSTRATIONS

COLOR

BLACK AND WHITE

Following page 72

INTRODUCTION

Persons close to the florist industry have realized for a long while that there has been a need for a popular-priced book on the subject of foliage plants. The amazing growth of this branch of horticulture continues to dazzle even those most closely associated with it. Modern homeowners first fell in love with the easy-to-grow Heartleaf Philodendron, and today it remains the most widely grown foliage plant. From that auspicious beginning indoor gardeners have clamored for an ever-increasing variety of "green plants," and men have searched jungles around the tropical world to satisfy this new longing for exotic house plants.

In a very real sense the plants being brought into commerce are new to ornamental horticulture. Even the most complete of the gardening encyclopedias of a decade ago fail to list many of the plants which now are among the most desired by flower lovers. This text endeavors, in down-to-earth language, to bring descriptive and cultural information about these new plants, as well as those which have stood the test of time.

Living plants add a subtle new dimension to our homes. Notice how many advertisements in today's magazines include in their pictures a lovely foliage plant or a bowl of flowers, no matter how prosaic the product they strive to sell. It is clearly recognized that living plants and flowers belong in every home. Advertisers simply capitalize upon the normal love of nature which lies within us all.

Foliage plants are easy to grow if one knows the rules that

apply to each plant. It is not enough to say "keep them warm and water them occasionally." These plants come to us from various parts of the world, and the degree to which we can duplicate their natural habitats spells the measure of our success with them in our homes.

I hope that you will allow yourself the pleasure of a home which abounds with the living splendor of growing plants. As you probably know, many types of foliage plants live for years before they become too large or ungainly for decorative use. The purpose of this text is to help you enjoy these living testimonies of the beauty of the earth for as long a time as possible.

J.U.C.

Concord, Massachusetts

FOLIAGE PLANTS FOR
INDOOR GARDENING

CHAPTER 1

YOU CAN GROW FOLIAGE PLANTS

TIMES HAVE CHANGED

How many times have you heard it said, "My grandmother used to grow Geraniums on every window sill, but I can't make one live in my house." There are good reasons why our grandmothers could grow certain plants which we find difficult, but have you ever stopped to consider that perhaps we can grow many plants that our forebears would have found impossible? We say, "Times have changed," but we do not always consider to what extent the climate in our homes has been altered by the advent of central heating. Today's generation of children is growing up in warm homes whose temperatures in midwinter are every bit as comfortable as those in the tropics. Gone are the days when kids used to scurry from the sanctuary of snug beds in unheated rooms to dress by the warm stove in the kitchen. Tropical plants would not have thrived under those Spartan conditions, although cool-loving Geraniums grew luxuriantly.

At the same time that heating engineers have been busy bringing tropical temperatures as close as our thermostats, architects have been designing homes and office buildings with wide expanses of glass. These two developments, dependable warmth and abundant light, set the stage for the greatest resurgence of interest in foliage plants in the history of horticulture. Even today plant hunters continue to press deeper into the little-known back country of forest-clad tropical mountains searching for new species. At home, huge ranges of greenhouses which formerly sheltered cool-growing, sun-loving flowering plants now prepare exotic foliage plants for market in a warm and humid twilight atmosphere reminiscent of the jungle.

Architects, aware of our basic need for beauty and of the sense of serenity engendered by living plants, have made indoor gardens an integral part of building designs. It is natural that architects should specify foliage plants, not only for their enduring grace and ease of maintenance, but because of the limitless choice of plant shapes, sizes, and leaf textures to be found among them. Interior decorators, consulting with florists, may choose from an array of foliage plants which range in size from creeping herbs to those of treelike dimensions.

All around us there is abundant evidence of the impact of foliage plants upon the commercial world. Every new shopping plaza, bank, office, and commercial building incorporates living plants into its décor. Those who deal in the esoterics of motivational behavior know that each of us responds to the lure of natural beauty; thus do merchants entice us to do business with them.

Until now the discussion has centered around buildings of contemporary design, but all of us do not live in new glass-walled homes either by choice or by chance, yet the foliage plant revolution has not passed us by. As a matter of record it should be said here that the abundance of light which pours through the sunny sides of some modern structures creates conditions which are actually too bright for many foliage plants. It ought to be more generally known that, in their native lands, most foliage plants begin life beneath the sheltering branches of older trees. They not only tolerate shade, but in most cases require protection from the full sun, especially when small. Thus it is that all homes have many places where foliage plants may be grown to perfection. The warmth of central heating which makes it difficult to succeed with many cool-loving flowering plants provides ideal conditions for green plants.

Finally, it must be apparent to every observant flower lover that some of the foliage plants they have seen appear to be unhappy. Perhaps this is to be expected until sufficient plant-care information is made available to those who select plants for various locations as well as those who ultimately are responsible for the culture of the plants. In addition, it should be said that relatively few persons know what one should expect from foliage plants. Their innate durability encourages many flower lovers to put up with plants which, though still alive, are no longer ornamental. Given proper care, foliage plants will last for months or years, depending upon many factors, but eventually they exhaust the nourishment in their pots, lower leaves fall, and the plants become straggly. Such plants cannot be rejuvenated. Even though repotted they will not send out fresh basal leaves. At such a time, do this: Count the number of months or years the plants have lent their beauty to your home, and be amazed at the return on your investment! It's time to replace the worn-out plants with fresh new ones.

This book has been planned to aid all persons concerned with the selection and care of foliage plants. It must be realized that the plants now in commerce come from various parts of the tropical world, and their indoor culture depends very much upon their origin. It is not enough to recall romantic movie scenes of waving Palms and warm sands and assume that all tropical plants are alike in cultural requirements. The climate of the tropics varies from humid jungles to cool rain forests to burning deserts. It is our good fortune that this is true because it assures us of a marvelous variety of plants from which to choose. At the same time it compels us to use our knowledge and common sense when selecting plants. No doubt you have seen plantings that combined desert Cacti with plants which require abundant moisture. Such incompatible groupings are all too commonplace. A study of the plants listed in this book, combined with reference to the exhaustive plant lists in the last chapter will enable you to choose foliage plants with intelligence and to care for them with an assurance of success.

A GLIMPSE AT THE WHOLE PICTURE

It would be fair to say that, once you have mastered the information contained in the balance of this chapter, you will have little, if any, difficulty growing foliage plants in your home. All such subjects as potting soil, atmospheric and soil moisture, plant foods, care of leaves, plants' light requirements, the effects of air conditioning, and the control of insects and diseases are covered thoroughly for plants in general. You might almost call this section a course in house plant culture. It is a guide by which you will be able to interpret the specific requirements of particular plants as they appear throughout the rest of the book. Never forget that all factors which affect the growth of plants are interrelated. You simply cannot overcome the lack of light by applying extra fertilizer. You cannot compensate for drought injury by applying water after injury has occurred. Remember that your pot plants have to depend upon you for all their needs. You will soon learn that the way of moderation is usually the best way to maintain foliage plants over long periods of time.

Perhaps you are a busy beginner in indoor gardening and haven't the time to ferret out all the plant-care information you would like to have. For you we have compiled the following brief suggestions. Like all generalizations, they are subject to exceptions, yet they contain much basic advice which will stand you in good stead.

1. Be an optimistic gardener. Never underestimate the ability of a plant to grow. Plants have been on earth longer than men.
2. Consider how little soil a flowerpot actually contains. You cannot neglect living plants without injuring them.
3. Learn to feed and water your foliage plants lightly so as not to encourage them to grow too large or too quickly.

4. Most foliage plants cannot tolerate direct sun, but thrive in bright shadows.

5. Foliage plants should not be put outdoors in the summer. The thin and delicate leaves they develop as house plants cannot cope with sun and wind and pelting rain.

6. High temperatures exhaust the strength of plants as well as men. Plants grown in air-conditioned rooms last longer than those grown in high temperatures. Most foliage plants last longest if grown at sixty-five to seventy-five degrees Fahrenheit.

7. Foliage plants can be kept at a given size for long periods of time if unwanted growth is removed as soon as it appears.

8. Face the fact that your plants will eventually become straggly or too large for their surroundings. Replace them with healthy young plants. We hope that this book will help you put this "day of discard" far into the future.

HOW TO WATER FOLIAGE PLANTS

It would be folly to suggest that there is a convenient set of rules by which one may learn how to water foliage plants. Indeed, the complexity of the subject may be easily grasped by taking into consideration only the fact that some plants come from deserts and others from tropical rain forests. This discussion is based, not on rules, but on the necessity of understanding how a plant's need for moisture is influenced by a number of external factors.

Of primary importance to a discussion of the moisture requirements of foliage plants is this question: What is the goal to be attained? This is a deceptively simple inquiry, for it would seem that one has only to answer that enough moisture should be given to keep the plants growing as they would in a greenhouse. This is far from the aim, however. The real objective of home culture is to maintain the health and beauty of foliage plants without increasing their size any more than is necessary. We surely do not want them to grow as fast as they do in a greenhouse, or they will soon become too large for our needs. There is a vast difference between watering for maintenance and watering for optimum growth.

Even the most carefully grown foliage plant has to undergo a period of adjustment as it is moved from a greenhouse to a home. For the first few weeks it will be necessary to give it comparatively more moisture than will be required later. When it has become acclimated to its new surroundings, the ideal amount of water to apply is just enough to keep the plant from suffering from lack of water. This is called "growing on the dry side" and is an old and established horticultural procedure. This bit of information has to be tempered by discretion, however. What is "on the dry side" for a moisture-loving plant might be too moist for a Cactus. Inform yourself of the needs of specific plants by consulting the text in later chapters.

It is only common sense to realize that plants grown in warm temperatures need water more often than those in cool ones. Likewise, plants in bright light use more water than their counterparts in dim light. Plants whose roots completely fill the pots and whose tops are large surely need moisture more often than do smaller plants whose roots have ample room to range in large pots.

The type of pot in which plants are grown has a large influence on the frequency of watering. An increasing number of foliage plants are being grown in plastic pots. Since plastic is impervious to water, there is little loss of moisture except from the soil surface and through the plants themselves. Clay pots, on the other hand, let both air and moisture through their sides; thus plants growing in them require considerably more water than those grown in plastic pots.

Plants grown in clay pots may be maintained more easily if the pots are set inside other containers which are at least two inches larger in diameter. The space between the pots should be filled with moist peat or sphagnum moss, or a combination of peat moss and perlite. After an initial adjustment period during which some moisture may have to be applied directly to the soil in the pots, all further water is put on the material between the pots. Its constant moisture is slowly absorbed through the walls of the clay pots, affording the plants a small but steady supply of moisture. This procedure is known as "double-potting." It may be practiced with plastic pots too, but its chief advantage under these conditions is to maintain a constant soil temperature. Water must be applied to the top of the soil as well as to the material between the pots, since there is no moisture interchange through plastic pot walls, but only through drainage holes at the base of each pot.

It is common practice to set potted plants inside decorative containers such as jardinieres. When this is done, extra care must be taken to determine that plants actually need water before more is given them. It is exceedingly easy to build up inadvertently a constant supply of water at the base of the container. This saturates the soil in the pot and eventually causes the plants to die.

In summary it should be said that watering is perhaps the most crucial operation connected with the care of foliage plants. The aim is to supply enough moisture so that plants never wilt, but not so much that they grow rapidly. Too little water causes root injury which eventually shows up in brown-margined leaves or outright death of plants. Too much water is the prime cause of leaf loss. A constantly saturated soil excludes oxygen so that roots cannot function properly and ultimately they decay.

SOILS FOR FOLIAGE PLANTS

You will find as you read this book that specific soil mixtures are suggested for many of the plants. These reflect the needs of the particular plants and will have already been met by the person who grew your plants until they became ready for retail sale. It should be said that any soil mixture must meet certain specifications if it is to satisfy the needs of foliage plants. Of these the primary one is that the soil must not become compacted, even after years of use. It must continue to be of open texture to allow air and water to enter and to encourage roots to roam freely. Such a mixture must be capable of holding a good deal of moisture upon which roots can draw as it is needed. It is not desirable that there be an abundance of fertilizer in the soil, for rapid growth is not wanted. Any food that is required may be added from time to time.

Many of the persons involved in horticultural experiments are working toward the standardization of a lightweight, spongy soil mixture that will meet the needs of most plants. One of the most popular today is composed of equal parts by volume of sphagnum peat moss and horticultural perlite. Perlite is an inert, sterile, nonnutrient, white silica material which combines light weight with great water-holding capacity. Since both the peat moss and the perlite have practically no food value, growers can add whatever is required. Another mixture uses equal parts of peat moss and vermiculite instead of perlite. Since vermiculite is made of mica which has been expanded through heat, it, too, contributes little food value. Each of these mixtures, starting with four quarts of sphagnum peat moss and four quarts of either perlite or vermiculite, should be enriched with one tablespoon of powdered 20 per cent superphosphate, two tablespoons of ground limestone, and four tablespoons of 5–10–5 fertilizer. It should be clear that these mixtures are still being tested and that home gardeners are apt to be more satisfied with the results obtained from traditional mixtures as set forth in later sections of this book.

THE PRACTICAL APPROACH TO PLANT FEEDING

In order to decide upon the amount of fertilizer to give foliage plants, one must first set forth the results that one wishes to accomplish. A commercial grower must, because of the expense involved in heating his greenhouse, endeavor to make his plants grow into salable sizes as quickly as possible. He uses the maximum amount of heat, moisture, food, and light that the plants can assimilate for optimum growth. On the other hand, the home gardener has nearly the opposite goal in view. He would like his foliage plants to stay within bounds as long as possible. He simply cannot follow the heavy feeding schedule of the commercial grower for two reasons: (1) he wants his plants to stay small; and (2) too much fertilizer under the dim light conditions of his home would kill the very plants he hoped to help.

Any house plant fertilizer which has given you good results when fed to other plants will serve to feed your foliage plants as well. Remember to use any fertilizer sparingly; too little is far better than too much. Never give plants more food than the amount recommended by the manufacturer. Either solid or liquid plant foods may be used, but in either case never apply them to plants when they are in need of moisture.

Fertilizer manufacturers are required to state an analysis of their product in the following order: (1) nitrogen; (2) phosphoric acid; and (3) potash. These figures appear as 5–10–5, 4–8–4, 23–19–17, or some other combination of three numbers. In each case they refer to the percentage of nitrogen, phosphoric acid, and potash included in the mixture. Although plants assimilate a great number of chemicals from the soil and atmosphere, these three are the ones usually needed to promote plant growth. When the term "a complete house plant fertilizer" is used, it refers to one which contains these three chemicals. Briefly, nitrogen fosters leaf growth, phosphoric acid induces sturdiness and rich colors, and potash stimulates root growth, thus each has a vital role to play in plant health.

You will find as you read this book that the amount of fertilizer recommended seems very small. It *is* small, but it is sufficient to maintain healthy foliage without fostering excessive growth. It must be remembered that many foliage plants will stay beautiful for years in your home if they are treated properly. Quite apart from their exotic qualities and the air of gracious living that foliage plants impart to a home is the fact that they are wonderfully inexpensive decorators if they are cared for properly. It is not at all uncommon for a plant which costs ten dollars, for example, to stay in beautiful condition for three years. This amounts to less than a penny a day and, of course, is one of the compelling reasons why foliage plants are so popular: They give high returns on small investments.

HUMIDITY AND HOUSE PLANTS

Special mention must be given to humidity, since the lack of moisture in the atmosphere of our homes can be a limiting factor to plant growth. Haven't you noticed that plants grow better when there are many of them than when there are but few? This is because plants constantly transpire moisture into the air about them, raising its relative humidity. A single plant might languish in a room, but if this plant were to be given a clear plastic cover to retain the atmospheric moisture, it would flourish. Persons who want to raise a few small moisture-loving plants find that the easiest way to do so is to buy or construct a glass-walled terrarium which might be called an indoor greenhouse. In essence, its only real contribution to plant health is to maintain a high degree of humidity in the air around the plants. This subject is covered more fully in Chapter 26.

Fortunately for indoor gardeners, many of the plants of the tropics are able to acclimate themselves to air which is drier than that which is optimum. In a sense this is a hidden blessing because plants will not grow as fast as they would if they had the full moisture and humidity of the jungle; thus they stay at a usable size longer. Such plants as Philodendrons, Rubber Trees, Australian Umbrella Trees, and others have smooth, hard-surfaced foliage which resists wilting and moisture loss; thus it is natural that we find some of the easiest to grow foliage plants among these families.

THE ROLE OF LIGHT IN PLANT GROWTH

All gardeners realize that plants cannot grow without light, yet we are not always aware of the subtle ways in which light influences growth through its interaction with other forces. For example, plants cannot assimilate fertilizer without sufficient light and experienced gardeners know that it is easy to over-water plants which are growing in dimly lighted locations. More basic, however, is the fact that vital growth processes within plants take place only when light reaches their leaves. Scientists have a name for the phenomenon by which green plants manufacture sugars and starches in their leaf cells. They call it *photosynthesis*, that is, "putting together in the presence of light." Natural or artificial light, falling on the green chlorophyll in leaves, is the basis of all life on earth.

Plants which grow in greenhouses have unrestricted daylight, but since our homes have roofs, our house plants have to get by with much less light. Those which grow at windows which face south or west get more sunshine and greater heat than those which grow at eastern or northern exposures. Overhanging eaves, porches, or trees drastically affect the amount of light which may reach house plants. In a sense, it is fortunate for indoor gardeners that we have so many places with varying degrees of light because, by choosing wisely, we may grow a wide selection of interesting plants. In Chapter 27 you will find long lists of plants which will thrive under differing light conditions.

No discourse on the subject of light and its effects on plants would be complete without a discussion of the way in which artificial light can supplement or take the place of natural light. Twenty-five years ago the author grew tropical plants in a below-deck storeroom of a Navy ship by simply keeping an incandescent light burning close to them for sixteen to eighteen hours each day. The science of *phytoillumination*, a big word meaning "to grow plants under artificial light," has made tremendous strides since that time. The whole industry of growing Chrysanthemums throughout the year, instead of in the autumn only, is based on schedules of lighting or withholding light from the plants at different stages of their growth.

Many other crops are brought into blossom out of season by the use of lights, but in this book we are more concerned with methods by which the health of foliage plants may be maintained in situations where natural light is deficient or totally lacking. It is perfectly amazing to see how well plants respond to supplementary light. Set a plant close to Dad's favorite armchair so that it will share part of the light shed upon his evening paper. Notice how luxuriantly foliage plants thrive in planter lamps which are turned on for a few hours each evening. One of the healthiest plants in our house is fifteen feet from the nearest window, but it sits beneath a bright standing lamp in the living room.

It can be said without equivocation that you can grow plants anywhere you want them provided you give them light. We recall remarking to a New Hampshire florist many years ago about his lovely African Violets. He said they were grown for him by a local nurse . . . under artificial lights in her cellar!

Growing plants under artificial light is not a gimmick. Electrical and agricultural engineers have done a lot of research on various light rays of the spectrum and the ways in which they influence plants. Many large-scale growers of plants start their seedlings under the controlled conditions of artificial light. In your home your supplementary light may be as simple as a table lamp or as complex as an automated "greenhouse" in your basement. In between these extremes are the lovely commercially available lighted stands and carts, some with multiple levels, in which one may grow beautiful plants without the aid of natural daylight.

It is interesting to know that plants grow best under the illumination of such research-inspired fluorescent lamps as Gro-Lux, Plant-Gro, and Plant-Lite. They do well when grown under ordinary fluorescent lamps too, and foliage plants will respond to ordinary incandescent lighting alone. If one does not choose to use such proprietary lamps as those named above, he will find that his plants will do very well under a combination of ordinary incandescent and fluorescent lamps when they are used at the ratio of one watt of incandescent to three watts of fluorescent. Foliage plants using artificial light alone should be given light for twelve to fourteen hours each day. Fertilizer for such plants should be very weak, not over one third the strength of that given to plants which grow in natural daylight.

Persons interested in more detailed information concerning this subject would do well to consult such a guide as *The Complete Book of Gardening Under Lights* by Elvin McDonald (Doubleday and Company, Inc., 1965).

AIR CONDITIONING AND ITS EFFECTS ON HOUSE PLANTS

How good it feels on an August day to step from the broiling sun into the luxury of an air-conditioned room! Those who work in air-conditioned offices and who live in air-conditioned homes are aware of the fact that they are less tired at the end of a day; they are not enervated; they do not have that "dragged-out" feeling.

There is a direct correlation between the health of plants and the well-being of humans in air-conditioned surroundings. Professor A. F. DeWerth of Texas A. &. M. University, after ten years of studies relating to the effects of air conditioning on plants, says:

The plants in our comparative trials in air-conditioned locations were always superior to those in uncooled areas during the summer months. We find that if the other environmental factors are controlled properly, the low humidities that prevail with air conditioning have no detrimental effects on those plants. Uniform temperatures are far more beneficial than uncontrolled ones.

Even in cool climates air conditioning is being built into nearly every commercial building, as well as a large percentage of private dwellings, and is, of course, an integral part of most buildings erected in warm climates. It is not hard to foretell that the occupants of such new housing will find it easy to grow both flowering and foliage plants.

In the discussion to this point we have been considering only so-called central air conditioning of homes and offices. These cooling systems are an integral part of the buildings themselves and operate so quietly and move great quantities of air so deftly that, except for the superb comfort level, one is seldom aware of the apparatus which brings about such an agreeable atmosphere. Protected as they are from the vagaries of nature, it is little wonder that plants prosper under this type of air conditioning.

Central air conditioning is in dramatic contrast to room air conditioning, which is defined as cooling performed by individual units set into wall or window openings. No doubt you have sat beside such a device until you simply had to move because of the cold air blowing across you. Perhaps the coolness of the breeze felt pleasant when you first entered the room, but its cumulative effect eventually began to make you feel chilly. It must be remembered that drafts of any kind have a depressing effect on house plants because they cause an excessive loss of moisture and, in addition, often actually chill plants to temperatures lower than they can withstand. An immediate effect may be wilting, but a more serious and lasting effect is the yellowing and loss of lower leaves. When one remembers that foliage plants are native to tropical parts of the world and cannot tolerate cold, it is easy to see that they should not be placed in the air stream of an air-conditioning system. This does not mean that rooms air-conditioned by window or wall units will not serve as fine places in which to grow foliage plants; it simply points out the common sense of setting the plants out of the blasts of cold air.

You might ask about the care of foliage plants during such periods as weekends when offices are closed and air-conditioning systems are not functioning. It is true that there will be a rise in temperature when cooling equipment is not in operation and a corresponding drop when it begins to take effect again. Yet, this change is so gradual, and it occurs at such long intervals that plants enjoy many more days of regularity than they do under the uncontrolled rise and fall of normal diurnal temperatures in homes and offices which are not air-conditioned during summer months.

It may come as a surprise to readers to learn that air-conditioned greenhouses have been used by the floral industry for many years. Summertime temperatures in uncooled greenhouses rise so high that many were left vacant part of the year, particularly in southern areas. Such flowers as Carnations and Chrysanthemums, both of which thrive in cool weather, now occupy greenhouse benches regardless of the season. Forced ventilation and evaporative cooling lowers greenhouse temperatures to such an extent that fine quality blossoms may be harvested even during the hottest days of the year.

In summary, remember that plants do better under the steady temperatures of air conditioning than they do when subjected to the normal high and low temperatures we can expect to encounter during our usual summer weather.

HOW TO CARE FOR THE LEAVES OF YOUR FOLIAGE PLANTS

Even at the risk of controversy, we feel that something should be said about the present fad of trying to make all leaves shiny. It seems perfectly clear that all plants are not alike; in fact, it might be said that diversity is in itself one of the charms of nature. Some plants have naturally glossy foliage which is a joy to see, but others have equally appealing silvery, deep green, gray-green, or fuzzy leaves which do not have a sheen. The immediate result of applying a preparation to such leaves is to give them an artificial appearance which may fool the uninitiated, but does not deceive any person who understands plants.

The long range effect is even more vital. It must be remembered that leaves are not on plants just for our enjoyment, but for the survival of the plants. Without leaves, plants quickly starve, for the conversion of natural elements into living matter takes place within leaf cells. Whatever we do to hinder the operation of the leaves slows down the growth of the plants.

Leaves are the breathing organisms of plants. The exchange of air and moisture is handled through certain remarkable surface cells known as *stomata,* which have the ability to open and close depending upon external conditions. Nearly all plants have these cells on the bottoms of their leaves, and many have them on the tops as well. Anything which keeps these cells from working properly, whether by clogging them with any substance, or by injuring them in any way, cuts down on their efficiency, thus stripping a plant of its food-manufacturing capacity. This is the long-range objection to coating leaves with any material to make them appear to be something which they are not. It is true that some plants, particularly those with hard-surfaced leaves, apparently will tolerate this treatment. Surely it cannot be construed as a benefit to plants to coat their leaves with a material to make them appear shiny. Whatever you do, *never use any kind of oil on the leaves of your plants.* (Do not confuse shiny leaf substances with foliar feeding. Foliar feeding is a means of giving nourishment to plants by applying a very dilute fertilizer and water mixture to the leaves. This is a proven method of plant feeding which does not coat leaves, but does give them a quick supply of food.)

Without exception, the best way to care for the leaves of your house plants is to wash them in clear tepid water. You can take them to the sink or into the bathtub or outdoors in mild weather. Wash the foliage with a gentle spray, or lacking that, wipe the leaves with a soft damp cloth. This kind of care will not only get rid of dust and give the leaves a natural appearance of health, but will wash most bugs right down the drain! Let the foliage dry in a place out of the sun because indoor plants have thinner and more delicate foliage than their outdoor cousins.

HOW TO KEEP FOLIAGE PLANTS WITHIN BOUNDS

In preceding sections of this chapter mention was made of the necessity of limiting the amount of food and moisture available to foliage plants so that they will not become too large for the space allotted to them. Certain of the herbaceous ones can be divided and repotted, giving several small plants in place of one large one, but basically, this size problem applies to plants which are either vines or incipient trees.

The essence of keeping plants within bounds is timeliness. Never let growth get so much out of bounds that you have to prune it off; instead, pinch it off when it is young and tender. By doing so you will force the plant to send out side growths which only add to its beauty and compactness. Members of the Philodendron family are good examples of plants which respond well to pinching. Never let them get long and straggly, but keep after those growths that want to stretch too far and remove them promptly.

Some of the larger-growing foliage plants, such as the treelike members of the *Ficus* family, pose quite a problem when it comes to keeping them small. They will respond to pinching as well as other plants do, but often the gardener is intrigued by the possibilities of growth within a plant and will let it go on and on until there is no recourse but to carry it away and begin with a younger one. The author admits to having been mesmerized by such an eagerly growing plant until it reached the ceiling!

CONTROL OF INSECTS AND DISEASES

Mention has been made of the efficacy of washing plants in clear water to rid them of insects. In these days of powerful insecticides it is easy to think that one should bring out his full armament to combat the smallest infestation. Generally, this is not at all necessary, provided a regular schedule of inspection and washing is followed. If such minor insects as aphids should appear on your plants, use a mild insecticide such as nicotine sulphate and a few soap flakes to ensure good coverage of the leaves. This is commonly sold under the name Black-Leaf 40. Malathion may be used for aphids, but it is quite toxic and its odor is so nauseous that one should treat plants outdoors rather than in the house. In addition to aphids, Malathion will kill red spider mites, mealy bugs, white flies, thrips, and most scale insects in their soft stage of growth. This list comprises more insects than you are ever likely to see on your house plants. Do not use Malathion on *Adiantum, Nephrolepis,* or *Pteris* Ferns or on *Crassula* species.

A more expensive but very easy method of insect control is offered by aerosol bombs developed specifically for house plants. Follow directions carefully. Stay back away from the plants and envelope them in spray mist. Be sure to read all labels carefully so as not to spray plants which may be injured by the ingredients in the spray mixture.

It is quite rare to find diseases on foliage plants, with the exception of rotting of roots and stems because of overwatering. As a general statement it can be said that few, if any, plants normally grown as house plants will thrive in a soil that is constantly saturated. Even those that enjoy a moist soil cannot tolerate stagnant water around their roots. Plants that are newly repotted, or that are weak, or that are growing in shady places must be watched carefully to see that they are not given too much water.

Should a leaf disease develop, resulting in spotting of foliage or appearance of soft wet areas on the leaves, the usual answer is to isolate the plants so the disease will not spread to others. The next step is to keep moisture off the leaves because this is the way in which most disease spores are spread. Also, it is true that moisture is necessary for diseases to grow, and dry leaves offer less opportunity for spores to germinate. The final control measure is to spray the leaves with a fungicide. Captan is a good one, readily available. Such sprays as are sold to combat leaf diseases of Roses may be found at any garden supply house. These will do the job too, but remember that most sprays of this type leave a residue on the foliage which may be objectionable. One obvious answer to the problem of a badly diseased plant is to discard it right away, pot and all, and begin anew with a younger and healthier plant.

VISUAL AIDS IN DIAGNOSING FOLIAGE PLANT PROBLEMS

Although plants cannot cry aloud, they have ways of telegraphing their distress by a number of eloquent signals. What is confusing to the "plant doctor" is that plants sometimes display the same indication of discomfort for more than one form of affliction. Just as a headache may come from something as simple as overindulgence or as serious as a brain tumor, plants may have more than one condition aggravating their wretchedness.

As we have mentioned previously, too much water can bring trouble to foliage plants. It is the primary cause of yellowing leaves, especially lower leaves. Yellowing foliage may also be caused by chilling or by leakage of artificial gas, but usually the problem can be traced to too much moisture. Water may have collected in the bottom of a jardiniere, for example, long enough to drown submerged roots. Be sure that your plants have good drainage.

Gardeners who have been too generous in the use of fertilizer should not wonder why the margins of leaves turn brown. It is really a type of burn which results when plants get more food than they can assimilate. Of course, a similar appearance may occur when plants have been deprived of moisture. If only the leaves on one side of a plant are brown, suspect physical injury by persons brushing against them, or sunburn from exposure to too much light.

Plants quickly react to insufficient light by stretching toward the light source and producing small leaves widely spaced on weak stems. Such plants may sometimes be salvaged by cutting off the straggly growth and at the same time moving the plant into a brighter location.

Certain plants have small leaves and seem to make little or no new growth. This is often caused by keeping the soil too dry, or by trying to grow the plants in hard soil such as that which one might get from his garden. Garden soil lacks sufficient organic material to withstand the compacting action of repeated waterings that house plants require.

Wilted leaves may mean that a plant simply needs a drink of water, but sometimes it occurs on plants which have been kept too wet. Under these conditions it is not surprising to find that roots have died due to their long immersion.

HOW TO RECOGNIZE GOOD QUALITY FOLIAGE PLANTS

The ultimate test of a good quality foliage plant from the point of view of the homeowner is this: Has the plant been grown in such a way that it will continue to thrive if given reasonable care under household conditions? *Should this one factor be lacking, all of the others are of little value.* It is futile to talk of lovely foliage and large plants for small prices if the plants are not likely to succeed. Once this basic assumption has been recognized, we are able to discuss the hidden attributes which determine real value.

There are ways to cut corners in nearly every type of endeavor, and horticulture is no exception. To the uninitiated two plants may appear very much alike. If the price tag on one plant differs widely from that on another plant of the same size and variety, a person is entitled to know what factors lie behind the price differential. A skilled eye can pick out the plant whose leaves are too far apart, whose growth has been so forced under conditions of heat and humidity that it cannot possibly cope with the drier air of an average home. He can pick out the plant which has not been "finished," one whose root system has not been given time to grow enough to support the plant in a home, although it does nicely in a moist greenhouse. Since time costs money, one plant may sell for more than another, although both look very much alike in all outward aspects. The more expensive plant may be truly the better bargain because its grower had the integrity to keep the plant in his greenhouse until it could safely be moved into home surroundings.

How are you going to know about such things? It takes years to learn how to judge quality plants. Our advice is simply this: If you are not a plantsman, then put your trust in someone who is. Your local florist has a reputation to maintain, and he cannot do it with poor merchandise. Perhaps every honest businessman suffers from time to time from what he knows is unfair competition, but florists seem to catch an extra load of grief because their customers, being unaware of unseen values, are tempted by price advertising. Your florist often gets (usually over the telephone) such questions as "Why did all the leaves drop off my Rubber Plant?" Sooner or later he learns to counter with another question, "Did you purchase the plant from me?" In nearly every case the answer is "No." Leaders in the floral industry continue to admonish growers not to fall into the trap of second-rate quality in order to sell at a cut-rate price, for they know that in the long run only those plants which grow successfully in our homes are worth while.

PLASTIC "FOLIAGE PLANTS"

It may seem incongruous that plastic plants should be discussed in a book such as this, which is devoted to the cultural requirements of live plants. Members of the floral industry were faced with this same dilemma when reasonably lifelike replicas of foliage plants first came on the market several years ago. In the beginning the battle lines were sharply drawn: Some implied that it bordered on sacrilege even to consider the use of artificial plants while others chose to sell what their customers seemed to want. As the years have passed and the so-called "permanent" plants have become more realistic in appearance, they have become part of the stock available in most florist shops.

It is noteworthy to mention that the appeal of plastic plants increases in proportion to their likeness to real plants. In a sense flower lovers are admitting that they would much rather have live plants, but since their success with live plants has been limited, they have had to settle for second best. It is the firm desire of the author that this book will help to fill the educational void which has kept persons from enjoying the true grace and beauty of living plants. In a way the difference between plastic plants and live ones may be likened to the difference between dolls and babies. As children we were fascinated by dolls, but as adults we realize their limitations and desire real children.

It must be admitted that there are locations which are so poorly suited for plant growth that it would be foolhardy to try to grow living plants. It is surely reasonable to have artificial plants under these conditions, and they do add attractiveness to the scene. They last for long periods of time, but it is a mistake to think that they remain attractive indefinitely. They gather dust, their colors fade, and they eventually look shopworn and need to be replaced, even as living plants do.

As a final thought about plastic foliage plants, it must be said that they are not inexpensive. Well-made ones cost a great deal more than living plants of the same size. Plastic plants are here to stay, but remember that their appeal depends upon their fidelity to nature. Remember, too, that you need not settle for artificial plants. Through the easy-to-follow instructions given in this book you can enjoy in your own home the incomparable living beauty of some of the most exotic plants known to horticulture, gathered from the far corners of the world.

DESIGNATION OF PLANT ORIGIN

It may be of interest to you to know that certain house plants are original species exactly like those which grow wild in some parts of the world. Most of the plants discussed in this book fall within this category, but some of them are hybrids, and in order to point them out, the letter *x* will appear before their names. It should be noted that all improved varieties are not of hybrid origin, but may be simply selections that have shown themselves to be somewhat better or different from the original type. Most variegated plants are in this group, as well as mutations which may be more vigorous or ornamental than the parent species.

ORDER OF IMPORTANCE

You may wonder why this book is organized as it is, rather than in a conventional alphabetical manner. The answer is that some families of plants are much more important as foliage plants than others. Those plants more apt to be of interest to indoor gardeners, or those with many attractive varieties, or those needing special culture are given special attention. Chapter 23, Minor Foliage Plants, contains cultural needs for a host of one-of-a-kind plants, many of which are excellent foliage plants, although not often grown primarily because their good qualities have not had sufficient publicity.

CHAPTER 2

RUBBER TREE RELATIVES
(*Ficus*)

It seems to this generation of flower lovers that Rubber Trees have always been with us. We can remember as children seeing them growing in restaurant, barbershop, and laundry windows. Most of the plants we saw were India Rubber Trees, whose glistening leaves and pink-tinted buds conjured up dreams of the tropics in our youthful minds. It is difficult to realize that it was only one hundred fifty years ago that English explorers first discovered wild India Rubber Trees growing in the hinterlands of Assam and Burma. At that time little thought was given to these trees as ornamentals, but the economic possibilities of their latex-bearing properties were quickly comprehended. Curiously enough, it is said that the first use of rubber was for the manufacture of erasers! Nowadays natural rubber is rarely drawn from India Rubber Trees, but from the sap of a Brazilian species known as *Hevea*.

Scattered throughout the tropics of the world are over six hundred different plant species related to the India Rubber Tree. Most of the ones grown as house plants bear the name Fig because our common edible Fig is the most famous member of the family. The botanical name for Fig is *Ficus*, and it is this Latin name by which they are recognized by plant lovers around the world. All members of the Fig family bear Figlike fruit, but much of it is woody and not edible.

We are not interested in this amazing plant family either for its fruit or for its rubber, but because it contains several nearly indestructible house plants. Nearly all are evergreen plants from tropical regions of the world, but they vary in size from creeping vines to enormous jungle trees that exceed one hundred feet in height. In India, for example, there is a Banyan Tree, *Ficus benghalensis*, which is said to have sheltered Alexander the Great and seven thousand of his men. It is still growing, and because of its singular ability to send down aerial roots which eventually become stems, this tree now has over three thousand trunks and is more than two thousand feet in circumference. Such inherent strength and longevity in a plant family are convincing evidence that its members ought to make tough house plants.

It should go without saying that Rubber Plants thrive in the warmth of our homes. In sections of the world where they can be grown outdoors they will tolerate nearly freezing weather during the dormant season, but they prefer the regular and constant warmth which is typical of their homelands.

One of the reasons this family of plants has maintained its popularity throughout the years is because of its tolerance of a wide range of light conditions. Ideally, its members should be given filtered light, but they will grow in full sun provided enough moisture is given them. They will even survive for long periods of time in dark locations, although they will eventually languish. Refer to the section in Chapter 1 regarding the necessary balance between light, moisture, and fertilizer.

Perhaps the most important cultural information we can give you about Rubber Plants is to make sure that the soil beneath them stays barely moist at all times. It should never dry out, nor should it remain saturated. Too much or too little water will cause the leaves to turn yellow and fall. If plants are in a cool position during the winter months, they will become partially dormant. They need less water during this resting stage than when they are in active growth.

Most house plants are of an ideal size when they are purchased from a florist. For that reason it is not advisable to give them a great deal of fertilizer. The goal is to maintain rich green foliage without fostering excessive growth. You will find that a mild feeding of any house plant fertilizer applied once every six months will be sufficient to keep your Rubber Plants healthy.

It is common knowledge among plant growers that members of the Rubber Plant family grow very well in pots which seem to be too small for them. Actually, they do better this way than when given large pots. Nevertheless, the time will come when your plants need to be repotted. If the job is too much for you, ask your florist for assistance; otherwise, use a humusy potting mixture made of equal parts of loam, peat moss, and sharp sand. This operation is best done in early spring just before new growth starts.

Upright growing species of Rubber Plants may become too tall for the spot you have chosen for them. Do not hesitate to prune them to suit your needs. The white latex which exudes from each cut will soon dry and harden, and new shoots will spring from leaf axils below the point of pruning. You may even want to experiment with air-layering* before pruning to see if you can start some new plants from the tips of your older ones.

The only care you should give the foliage of your Rubber Trees is to wipe the dust off the leaves occasionally with a soft damp cloth.

Ficus australis variegata, see *Ficus rubiginosa variegata*

Ficus benghalensis, Banyan Tree

The ease with which the common India Rubber Tree, *Ficus elastica*, can be grown has encouraged plantsmen to bring into house culture many of the other members of the family. This species does not have shiny leaves, but the new foliage and stems have an abundance of pinkish hairs which make them

---

* A method of propagation, employed with certain plants whose branches cannot be brought to the ground for layering, in which a portion of a branch or stem, sometimes girdled, is kept covered, by wrapping with moist moss, then plastic, until it forms roots and may be detached from the parent and planted.

very attractive. Its broadly elliptical leaves are four to eight inches long. As noted above, the Banyan becomes a large tree in its native India.

Ficus benjamina, Weeping Fig

The Weeping Fig has become a very popular indoor plant where there is room to display it properly. Most specimens are grown as single-stem trees to heights of four to six feet, at which point the top growth is allowed to form a dense head of gracefully weeping foliage. Leaves are slender, four to six inches long, and shiny. This plant is native to India and Malaya.

Ficus benjamina exotica, Java Fig

This species is a particularly graceful weeping type very much like *F. benjamina* except that the ends of the new growth exhibit a characteristic twist. It is native to parts of Indonesia.

Ficus carica, Common Fig

It is surprising to see the number of northern gardeners who cherish a tub-grown Fig tree. Unlike other plants mentioned in this section, the Common Fig is deciduous and loses its leaves during the winter months. It can be stored in a cold but not freezing place in the fall, then brought into the house in mid-winter, where it will soon send forth new leaves and even fruit if given sunshine.

Ficus diversifolia (*F. lutescens*), Mistletoe Fig

This plant gets its name from the fact that its dull, roundish leaves look much like Mistletoe foliage. It bears a quantity of small, round, yellowish fruit, even on young plants. It is a small shrub in its native Malaysia, thus remains a small plant in cultivation. Most house plant specimens vary from eight inches to two feet in height.

Ficus elastica, India Rubber Tree

In the opening paragraph of this discussion of Rubber Tree relatives we were talking about the original species of *Ficus elastica*. This particular Rubber Tree is not grown in great quantities nowadays because several of its varieties make more beautiful house plants. Although there are many horticultural selections, only the better ones are listed below.

Ficus elastica decora (See Plate 1.)

This wonderful variety of Rubber Tree is said to have originated as a chance seedling in Indonesia several years ago, where it quickly captured the imagination of gardeners. Its leaves are longer and often more than twice as wide as those of its parents. Mature leaves are broadly oval, being six inches or more wide, and twelve or more inches long. They are thick, heavy, and of a deep glossy green. The midvein of each leaf is ivory colored above and red beneath, and the protective sheath that encloses each new leaf is bright red. In fact, the ruddy hue is apparent throughout this plant, as well as in the variety *rubra*, contributing to the richness of its foliage. Each new leaf unfolds, not green, but with the color and appearance of burnished bronze.

Ficus elastica doescheri

For many years the only *F. elastica* with colored foliage was the one known as *variegata*, but it has been superseded by the brighter *doescheri*, whose foliage is marked by areas of white, cream white, and gray, with pink midribs and leaf petioles. It should be remembered that most plants with variegated leaves are not as easy to grow as their green-foliaged cousins.

Ficus lutescens, see *Ficus diversifolia*

Ficus lyrata (F. pandurata), Fiddle-Leaf Fig (See Plate 2.)

The Fiddle-Leaf Fig is native to the sultry western coast of tropical Africa. There it becomes as much as forty feet tall, but as a potted plant its growth can be restricted to the needs of the gardener. Its beauty lies in its tremendous shiny, leathery, fiddle-shaped leaves which measure twelve to eighteen inches in length and persist on the plant for years.

Ficus nitida, see *Ficus retusa nitida*

Ficus pandurata, see *Ficus lyrata*

Ficus panduriformis, see *Ficus wildemanniana*

Ficus parcellii, Clown Fig

In recent years a few specimens of the interesting Clown Fig have come into commerce. Its name comes from the fact that its hairy leaves and even its tiny green-to-red marble-shaped fruit are marked with streaks and blotches of white. Its thin leaves are four to six inches long and half as wide and are toothed along the margins. The Clown Fig is native to the islands of the South Pacific.

Ficus pumila (F. repens, F. stipulata), Climbing or Creeping Fig

Perhaps you have seen this plant many times without realizing that it was a Fig. It is commonly grown in warm greenhouses or outdoors in mild climates. Its one-inch leaves are heart-shaped and dull green in color. They cling closely to the stems, which send out aerial roots as they climb moist walls in shady places.

Ficus radicans variegata (F. rostrata variegata), Variegated Rooting Fig

There is a plain-foliaged Rooting Fig, of course, but the brightly marked white and green leaves of this type make it the more popular of the two. Its narrow leaves are two to four inches long and are pointed at the ends. This plant is a good selection whenever a trailing plant is needed for a basket or indoor planter.

Ficus repens, see Ficus pumila

Ficus retusa nitida (F. nitida), Indian Laurel

Indian Laurels are usually grown in the same treelike habit as are *Ficus benjamina* specimens, and they have much the same over-all appearance, except that their branches grow in an upright manner instead of weeping. Their waxy dark green leaves are elliptical in shape and about three inches long.

Ficus rostrata variegata, see Ficus radicans variegata

Ficus rubiginosa variegata (F. australis variegata), Variegated Rusty Fig

Queensland, Australia, has contributed this very attractive member of the Rubber Tree family, whose small oval deep green leaves are elegantly edged and blotched with generous areas of creamy yellow. It is an excellent foliage plant, not only for its color, but because its leaves are not large and stiff, as is often the case with varieties of *F. elastica*. For that reason this species has a refined appearance which will surely contribute to its popularity as it becomes better known.

Ficus stipulata, see *Ficus pumila*

Ficus wildemanniana (*F. panduriformis*)

This species from the African tropics is relatively new to commerce, but has interesting possibilities. It has a habit of branching when quite small, making a full little plant with shiny, dark green, leathery leaves marked by ivory-colored veins.

CHAPTER 3

PHILODENDRONS ARE FOR EVERYONE

Where does one begin or stop in describing the Philodendron family? Well over two hundred species have been found in the jungles of Central and South America, and there is no doubt but that still others will come to light as remote jungle areas are combed for new and different plants. To these must be added the many fine new Philodendron hybrids coming into commerce in increasing numbers.

Perhaps the most familiar foliage plant in America today is the common Heartleaf Philodendron. It is hard to conceive that there are other members of the family with single leaves seven feet long on plants which become treelike in habit and even have thorny trunks. While it is true that some Philodendrons have arboreal tendencies, this enormous family is composed chiefly of climbers. They work their way upward through the jungle twilight by clambering from branch to branch, sending down long aerial roots which eventually reach to the ground. It is easy to see how some of them get started in the wet leaves gathered in the crotches of old trees, or on moist decaying branches high above the ground. In such locations they may grow for years before their roots reach solid ground.

A certain number of Philodendrons are of the type known as self-heading. One could say that they grow like cabbages, with all of their leaves arising from a central crown. It is easy to see how valuable such plants can be as decorators, for they rarely grow too large for their surroundings, though it must be admitted that many of them are large plants by nature and must be given plenty of room so as to be seen at their best. By combining these true self-headers with vining types, hybridists have come up with plants with smaller foliage and definite restraint in their desire to climb.

All Philodendrons grow best in a soil that is of high humus content. Some commercial growers use pure peat moss, but more of them add as much as one third or one half sharp sand or perlite. A soil composed of one third each of rich loam, peat moss, and sand will suit them also. The important thing to remember is that they thrive in a highly organic soil.

In greenhouses it is common practice to feed Philodendrons every three or four weeks to make them grow as fast as possible, but in the home three feedings a year of a complete house plant fertilizer will suit their needs.

"How often should I water my Philodendrons?" seems to be a common question. It can be answered this way: No matter how you water them, the first requisite is that the soil be well drained so that it will not become saturated with moisture. Once this factor is understood, it might be said that the frequency of watering will determine the rate of growth to a large extent. In house culture the soil can be allowed to become barely dry on the surface before more water is applied. Do not allow your plants to wilt, but do maintain them "on the dry side" to suppress exuberant growth.

Philodendrons are ideal plants for poorly lighted spots in your home, for by nature they are accustomed to the dim light of forests. They do best where there is an abundance of indirect light, but no sun. They will endure dark locations for extended periods of time, but if they are given supplementary artificial light, they will continue to grow indefinitely.

Philodendron leaves do not need any other care than an occasional wiping with a damp cloth to remove dust.

It is not practical to include in the following section all of the Philodendrons that you could grow in your house. Instead, the list will be restricted to the better ones which are available in florist shops today. No florist will have all the varieties mentioned, but likewise, no florist will fail to have at least one kind of Philodendron. It is well to know why certain varieties have been excluded, for example, the gorgeous *P. andreanum* and the exotic *P. verrucosum*. These species, as well as some others, simply do not thrive outside of the rich humidity of a warm greenhouse. It is interesting to know that many species of Philodendrons have mutations with mottled green and white foliage. These usually do not grow as lustily as the green-leafed types and are not always as pretty as one might imagine.

Perhaps a word should be said about the lack of common names for many of the newer Philodendrons. As a matter of fact, as far as commercial growers are concerned, common names are too ambiguous. They must be certain that the plants they receive are the ones they order; so they cling to botanical names that signify only one species. The ultimate consumer usually relies upon the recommendation of his florist and doesn't usually care too much about English names as long as the plants do well. Thus, except in rare instances, common names are never coined.

CLIMBING PHILODENDRONS

The very name *Philodendron* comes from the Greek words *philos*, "loving," and *dendron*, "tree," and refers to the nature of most species to climb or lodge among the trees of the jungle. In house culture these plants may be allowed to climb a support or to trail over the side of a flowerpot, hanging basket, or mantel. A strange phenomenon you may notice is that the leaf size usually increases whenever a Philodendron is allowed to climb. The supports may be rough-barked slabs of wood, mossy posts, or "totem poles" of Tree Fern fiber. If they are moistened occasionally, the plants will grow faster and will soon cling to the uprights with aerial roots.

x *Philodendron* Burgundy

This well-known hybrid is said to contain the "blood" of four different wild species. It is a delightful plant with arrowhead-shaped leaves as much as twelve inches long. They are a deep green with wine-red undertones and have rich burgundy-colored stems, leaf petioles, and new buds.

Philodendron cordatum (*P. oxycardium*), Heartleaf Philodendron (See Plates 6 and 25.)

As so often happens in horticulture, a plant acquires a name somewhat different from its correct one, but no one except the experts ever make much of a fuss about it. Such a plant, so beloved by millions, is our common Heartleaf Philodendron. Its real botanical name is *oxycardium*, but it is better known as *cordatum*. It has an intriguing history, having been first found by Captain Bligh of *Mutiny on the Bounty* fame and brought by him from Jamaica to England, from whence it spread abroad to become the most commonly grown foliage plant in the world. It has been the plant which, by its thriving, has encouraged untried indoor gardeners to enlarge their scope to include a wider range of house plants. The Heartleaf Philodendron will grow in clear water, as well as in a soil mixture. Put the long ends of your vines into a vase and watch them grow.

Philodendron dubium (*P. dubia*)

There is a decided difference in the shapes of leaves of certain plants, depending upon whether they come from young or mature specimens. The Philodendrons sold as *dubium* or *dubia* are really juvenile plants of the true *P. radiatum*, a strong-growing climber from Guatemala and southern Mexico, known for its large, deeply lobed leaves. The young plants seen in greenhouses and flower shops have large leaves, but very shallow lobes. As the plants mature, particularly if they are allowed to climb a support, they produce more deeply incised leaves.

x *Philodendron* Florida (See Plate 4.)

You could search the jungles of the world in vain for the magnificent *Philodendron* Florida, because it is a hybrid which was developed in a Florida greenhouse between the Peruvian species P. *laciniatum* and P. *squamiferum,* from the humid jungles of Guiana on the eastern coast of South America. One glance at a Florida Philodendron will convince you of the success of this hybridizing project. Those glossy, deeply lobed leaves accentuated by their fuzzy red petioles offer indoor decorators a uniquely beautiful foliage plant with all the qualities of toughness and tolerance which have made the Philodendron family name synonymous with ease of culture. Since this is a climbing type, it does best when given a support, but it will also grow beautifully when allowed to trail from a mantel, wall container, or from a hanging basket. The more closely knit variety P. Florida *compacta* has less of a tendency to climb.

Philodendron hastatum, Spear-Leafed Philodendron (See Plate 3.)

Botanical names should not bother you, for once you know their meaning, they can be very helpful. For instance, P. *hastatum* gets its name from the Latin word for spear, *hasta.* In other words, this is simply the Philodendron whose leaves are shaped like spearheads. From our point of view, it is important to know that this plant is very retentive of its thick-textured, glossy leaves. They will cling to the plant for years if it is given a well lighted spot. As an aside, it should be noted that many Philodendrons have spear-shaped leaves, but presumably only one of them could get the name.

Philodendron micans

If you have noticed a Philodendron which looks like the common Heartleaf species, except that its foliage is a shimmering silky bronze above and rusty red beneath, then you have already met P. *micans*. This is a rather strange little species, and botanists are not entirely sure but that it is a juvenile-leaved form of the Heartleaf Philodendron. At any rate, it is very beautiful, but not as easy to grow. It seems to like somewhat more warmth and humidity than the Heartleaf Philodendron, and it must be kept out of cold drafts.

Philodendron panduraeforme (P. bipennifolium), Fiddle-Leaf Philodendron

The imaginative gentleman whose task it was to choose a botanical name for this plant was inspired by the pandura, a romantic stringed instrument similar to the mandolin, used by Egyptian and Assyrian lovers in ancient days. Since its leaves are somewhat violin shaped, it has acquired the common name of Fiddle-Leaf Philodendron.

This species is a climbing plant from the humid jungles of southern Brazil, and because of the leathery texture of its leaves, it has shown a remarkable adaptability to house culture. Although it is usually grown against a slab of bark, it can be trained as a low, bushy plant by pinching out the ends of the stems.

Philodendron pertusum, see *Monstera deliciosa,* Chapter 17

Philodendron radiatum, see *Philodendron dubium*

SELF-HEADING* OR NEARLY SELF-HEADING PHILODENDRONS

x *Philodendron* (*P. auriculatum* x *P. imbe*)

This popular hybrid has a unique upright manner of growth, with narrow bright green leaves which become twelve to fifteen inches in length. It is not a true self-header, but it does have such a compact habit that it fits within this category.

Philodendron cannifolium

Like the preceding hybrid, this species from Guiana is a very short-jointed plant, although not a true self-header. Its leathery, narrowly elliptical leaves, ten to twelve inches long, are broad spreading and are borne on fat petioles which look much like the stalks of Water Hyacinths or the pseudobulbs of certain Orchids.

Philodendron "Espirito Santo," see *Philodendron williamsii*

x *Philodendron* Lynette

Most Philodendrons have rather smooth leaves, but this attractive hybrid has amazingly "quilted" foliage because each of the transverse veins on the leaves is deeply indented. The leaves themselves are tongue shaped, ten to fifteen inches long, and arise from a central crown to give somewhat the same appearance as a Bird's Nest Fern.

Philodendron melinonii

Guiana is the home of this interesting self-heading Philodendron, whose trowel-shaped, leathery light green leaves are offset

* Having leaves which arise from basal crowns or very short stems, as contrasted with common climbing or trailing species of Philodendrons whose leaves are borne along their stems.

by fat bright red leafstalks. This species is relatively new to commerce, but should become increasingly popular.

Philodendron selloum (See Plate 5.)

This large-growing self-heading Philodendron is native to that part of Brazil close to where the new capital of Brasilia has recently been built amid the rich forests of the interior. *P. selloum* is often used as a garden subject in the warmer parts of Florida and California, but its most important use is that of a superb house plant. Its large dark green leathery leaves are deeply lobed in young plants and become bipinnate* in older specimens.

x Philodendron Weber's Self-Heading

Although this hybrid is called a self-header, it is really a very short-stalked trailing or climbing type, yet it grows so compactly as to fall within the self-header category. Its leaves are narrowly elliptical, eight to twelve inches long, well spread out to make a very attractive house plant that will stay beautiful for a long while.

Philodendron wendlandii

The Central American countries of Costa Rica and Panama are home to this wonderful truly self-heading Philodendron. Its growth habit is that of a dense rosette made up of long, tongue-shaped, waxy green leaves, each of which is ten or more inches in length. Mature plants require considerable space to expand to their full beauty. This species is one of the best of the self-heading Philodendrons.

* Having leaf segments arranged feather-fashion.

Philodendron williamsii

A large area is needed to display the remarkable *P. williamsii*, known also as Espirito Santo, named for the Brazilian state of Espirito Santo, just north of Rio de Janeiro. Its special feature is the shape of its narrow, wavy-margined leaves, which become as much as three feet in length and look like enormous elongated spear points.

CHAPTER 4

THE AUSTRALIAN UMBRELLA TREE
(Schefflera)

It is easy to wax enthusiastic about the Australian Umbrella Tree. Even the name is an intriguing one, and no doubt comes from the fact that a single leaf of a jungle specimen is large enough to shield one from the sun, if not the rain. House-grown plants have the same exotic foliage, but they are not of such bold dimensions. Botanists say that each leaf is digitately compound because its various leaflets arise from a central point, just as our fingers spread out from the palms of our hands. A familiar native plant with similar foliage is Virginia Creeper. Schefflera foliage is not only attractive in shape, but is blessed with a naturally glossy surface which enhances its beauty.

There are three species of Schefflera (also known as Brassaia) which are grown in this country. The most important one for house culture is S. actinophylla (See Plate 7.), a native of the rain forests of Queensland, Australia, as well as New Guinea and Java. Recently a superb green-and-white-leafed type has been found and given the name S. actinophylla variegata. Two other species are less often grown as house plants, but are common in gardens in semitropical areas. They are S. digitata from New Zealand and S. venulosa from India.

The supreme attribute of Australian Umbrella Trees as house plants is that they will tolerate adversity. They will grow in bright light or full sun, as well as in areas where illumination is dim. This is true of many jungle plants which must survive in the shade until they are tall enough to find a place for themselves in the sun. Generally speaking, Australian Umbrella Trees will do best for you if you give them bright light, but not full sun.

In the humid heat and moisture of the jungle these trees grow rapidly, but fast growth is not usually the goal of home gardeners. Fortunately, Australian Umbrella Trees withstand the dry air and artificial heat of our homes without flinching. If these conditions help to keep them from outgrowing their indoor locations, all the better. At any rate, the only care the leaves need is an occasional washing or sponging with a damp cloth to remove dust.

Water your *Schefflera* plants well, then wait until the surface of the soil is nearly dry before giving them more moisture. This will not only keep them healthy, but will keep them from becoming too large. Be frugal about feeding your plants. A mild feeding of a complete house plant food every six months is sufficient to maintain health.

Australian Umbrella Trees will live for years in small flowerpots, but eventually they should be shifted to larger ones. Use a humusy soil mixture similar to the following: two parts loam, two parts leaf mold or peat moss, two parts sharp sand, one-half part dried cow manure, and a dusting of bone meal.

One last word about Australian Umbrella Trees points up another feature of interest to indoor gardeners. Plants which are not in active growth will tolerate near-freezing conditions, although they will not make new growth until the return of warm temperatures. If you are looking for a striking foliage plant that does not need to be pampered, try an Australian Umbrella Tree.

CHAPTER 5

GOLD AND SILVER POTHOS
(Scindapsus)

The story is told about a man who, perceiving the coming of World War II during the 1930s, decided to find the most remote tropical island in the Pacific and retire to this spot. Fate traveled with him, however, for he chose one of the Solomon Islands as his new home. What a sense of frustration he must have felt when some of the most intense fighting of the Pacific war swirled about him as Japanese and Allied fighting men converged on his island. Graying veterans today remember the heat and the jungle vines, but surely few of them remember the plants as being ornamental.

Among the most prevalent vines of southern Pacific islands is the one under discussion here. Botanists point out that its correct name is *Scindapsus aureus*, but it has been called Golden Pothos for so many years that this name is more familiar to indoor gardeners. Actually, there is a related species correctly known as *Pothos*, but it is rarely grown as a house plant. The original species, *Scindapsus aureus* (See Plate 8.), has dark green foliage attractively marked with yellow marbling. The heart-shaped leaves on mature plants may be two feet long and nearly as wide. This type of plant is being grown to an ever greater extent in this country, but under pot culture maximum foliage size is more apt to be ten to twelve inches. However, the real joy of this variable species is in its smaller leaved forms, whose foliage varies from two to four inches in length. In addition to the golden type there are many selections with markings of nearly pure white, as well as various shades of cream or yellow. Varietal names include Marble Queen, Orange Queen, Caribbean Yellow, Silver Moon, Tricolor, and Wilcox's Pothos. They are also known under such names as Devil's Ivy, Hunter's Robe, and Arum Ivy.

A second species of Pothos, *Scindapsus pictus*, and its variety *S. pictus argyraeus* are often called Silver Pothos because their soft green leaves are marked and edged with silvery gray.

All Pothos have one thing in common besides their botanical kinship: They thrive under the warm household conditions that most of us call comfortable. Unlike their relatives, the Philo-dendrons, Pothos like to dry out considerably between waterings. Let them get quite dry before giving them more water, especially during the winter months or when they are grown in shady locations. They respond to any ordinary house plant fertil-izer and will grow rapidly if given abundant light and mild feedings every month or so. Most indoor gardeners will do better, however, to feed them no more often than once every three or four months. They will grow beautifully in pure peat moss or in a humusy mixture of equal parts of peat moss, loam, and sand.

Pothos exhibit their brightest colors when there is ample light, although they should have protection from the full sun. Shade tends to subdue the colorful leaf markings.

As decorative plants, Pothos do beautifully when allowed to climb on bark slabs or other "totem poles": They make fine ground covers in planter boxes and are especially attractive as trailing plants in wall or hanging containers. They will stand drier air and warmer temperatures than many plants, but they resent chills, drafts, and constant moisture about their roots.

CHAPTER 6

HAWAIIAN TI
(Cordyline)

An ancient Hawaiian recipe might well have read, "Take one old dugout canoe; into it crowd several armloads of Ti, well bruised by flaying on a rock; add water, then let the mixture ferment for a few days." The resulting liquor, according to early visitors to the Sandwich Islands, was extremely potent. Englishmen soon learned to make a pleasant beer from the Ti's woody stems, as well as to boil down the sap to a fine-tasting sweet brown syrup. More romantically minded readers will relish the thought that hula skirts are made of Ti leaves!

Hawaiian Ti, known botanically as *Cordyline terminalis* (See Plate 9.), is a wonderfully effective foliage plant whose leaves by nature vary from deep green through many shades of pink and red. The varieties grown commercially were chosen for their particularly bright colors. As might be expected, the hues become more brilliant when the plants are exposed to an abundance of light, but they should be shielded from the full force of the sun. A favorite brightly colored selection is called Tricolor.

Ti plants grow best in an organically rich, moist soil. A mixture composed of equal parts of rich loam, peat moss, and sharp sand will suit them very well. Aim for an evenly moist but not saturated soil. You will find that Ti plants will do best for you if you provide a humid atmosphere, as well as a moist soil. Often this can be achieved by growing them in company with other plants in a tray underlaid with moist sand, peat moss, or other material which will aid in the evaporation of water into the air about the plants.

The early botanical records of Hawaiian Ti make intriguing reading. The *Edwards Botanical Register* of London, for example, in 1836 published an interesting account of the plant and its uses. In addition to a beautiful engraving of "The Sandwich Island Tee-Plant," mention was made of how useful mariners on the Pacific would find the plant, for it was an excellent forage for cattle and swine aboard the sailing vessels. It went on to describe how to prepare the roots for cooking and told of how the natives not only made clothes and thatched their huts with its leaves, but also accepted a Ti branch as an emblem of peace and carried it during interisland warfare as a flag of truce.

Although we write here of the Hawaiian Ti as a living foliage plant, many readers will recognize the fact that flower arrangers have long used its colorful foliage to add an exotic touch to their bouquets.

We offer the following testimony about Hawaiian Ti. During World War II at Pearl Harbor the writer was given a section of Ti stem, locally called a "log." Eighteen months later when he was transferred to another ship, the plants which sprouted from the log were still growing luxuriantly in a dish of plain water in a below-deck storeroom lighted only by an incandescent lamp. Is it any wonder that we recommend Hawaiian Ti as a tough house plant?

Another species of *Cordyline* is used ornamentally as the center attraction of urn plantings, for example, or in window boxes among annuals. This is *C. australis*, but is sold by florists as *Dracaena indivisa*. Each young plant is composed of a dense cluster of long, narrow, flat, arching bronze-green leaves.

CHAPTER 7

DRACAENAS OF CENTRAL AFRICA

The "white man's season" (October to April) was one of the time divisions used by early traders and explorers of the west coast of mid-Africa. Equatorial heat and some of the heaviest rainfall in the world combined to make the climate of this area inhospitable to all but the hardiest souls. It is in this part of the world that many Dracaenas are native. At least one species was discovered as long ago as 1768, but it remained for the awakening of interest in horticulture during Victorian days and the coming of age of central heating in homes to bring these exotic tropical plants into general commerce.

It is easy to realize that Dracaenas are good house plants because they need the warmth which we find comfortable. Even though the air may be drier than optimum for rapid growth, the plants nevertheless do very well in our homes and can be relied upon to last for long periods of time with relatively little care.

Dracaenas do best in a location where they will receive filtered light, but not full sun. They will thrive under artificial light if natural daylight is not available. Since they come from a part of the world where rainfall is heavy, it is easy to understand that the soil beneath them should stay moist at all times. A moisture-retentive soil mixture may be made of equal parts of rich loam, peat moss, and sharp sand. If it is enriched with a dilute house plant fertilizer once every six months, there will be enough nourishment to keep house-grown Dracaenas healthy.

The following species and varieties of Dracaenas are not the only ones grown, but they are among the most suitable for house culture. One or more of them is to be found in nearly any florist shop. You will appreciate care-free Dracaenas; make a place for them in your home.

Dracaena deremensis varieties

Several selections and mutations of the species *D. deremensis* are popular house plants. In general it might be said that they are upright-growing plants with long, broad, gracefully arching leaves, either dark green in color or marked with white or creamy yellow on a green background. Particularly good ones are: *bausei,* whose green leaves are marked by two white stripes narrowly separated by a green mid-line; Janet Craig (See Plate 11.), a variety with robust, gleaming dark green foliage; Roehrs Gold, a beautiful type with a very broad center line of creamy yellow on each leaf which is bordered by narrow white lines, and margined in green; and *warneckei,* a long-time favorite discovered at the turn of the century in what was then German West Africa by Heinrich Engler, the director of the Berlin Botanic Garden. It has luxuriant green foliage marked with slender whitish lines in the middle of each leaf, edged in turn by a band of white and finally by a margin of green.

Dracaena draco, Dragon Tree

In 1868, in the Canary Islands, a Dragon Tree estimated to be over six thousand years old was blown over in a storm. Such tenacity to life is an inborn characteristic of many Dracaenas and is one of the reasons they make such good house plants. This particular species, *D. draco,* is also the source of a reddish powder used by engravers, appropriately known as "dragon's blood." Although Dragon Trees may attain considerable height in the course of years, most cultivated specimens are relatively

PLATE 1

Ficus elastica decora, variety of India Rubber Plant

Ficus pandurata, Fiddle-Leaf Fig

PLATE 2

PLATE 3

Philodendron hastatum, Spear-Leafed Philodendron

Philodendron hybrid, Florida Philodendron

PLATE 4

Philodendron selloum, species of Philodendron

Philodendron cordatum, Heartleaf Philodendron

PLATE 5

PLATE 6

PLATE 7

Schefflera actinophylla, Australian Umbrella Tree

Scindapsus aureus, Golden Pothos

PLATE 8

PLATE 9

Cordyline terminalis tricolor, Hawaiian Ti

Dracaena marginata, Red-Margined Dracaena

PLATE 10

PLATE II

Dracaena deremensis Janet Craig, Janet Craig Dracaena

Dracaena fragrans massangeana, Massange Dracaena

PLATE 12

PLATE 13

Dracaena godseffiana Florida Beauty, Florida Beauty Dracaena

Dieffenbachia exotica, Exotic Dumb Cane

PLATE 14

PLATE 15

Dieffenbachia picta Rudolph Roehrs, Rudolph Roehrs Dumb Cane

Fatshedera lizei, Tree Ivy

PLATE 16

small. However, the cluster of thick, gray-green, swordlike leaves which arises from the end of each stem may easily be three to four feet across; so these plants are more suited to plantings in large public buildings than in homes.

Dracaena fragrans massangeana, Massange's Dracaena (See Plates 12 and 25.)

Massange's Dracaena is considered to be one of the finest of foliage plants. It has long, broad, deeply arching foliage of rich green marked with longitudinal stripes of lighter green and yellow. Most specimens of this plant are grown as ordinary compact house plants, but many are sold as upright "standards." In this growth habit all of the foliage arises from the top of a stalk in the manner of a Palm, but the "trunk" of the little "tree" is usually clothed with a climbing vine such as Heartleaf Philodendron.

The variety *victoriae* is not as suited to house culture, but is sometimes grown in warm conservatories. Its leaves have broad stripes of silvery gray, cream, and golden yellow.

Dracaena godseffiana Florida Beauty (See Plate 13.)

Dracaena godseffiana is surely one of the most striking plants to be found in nature in any part of the world. This member of the Lily family, whose broad whorled leaves are mottled with creamy-white areas and are borne on bushy plants, is most unlike a Lily in habit of growth. From this wild species has come, in this country, the variety Florida Beauty, in which the yellow-and-white foliage markings are much brighter than in the original form. Plants are low growing with thin, wiry stems and very persistent, tough, leathery foliage set in close-ranked pairs or whorls of three. Most plants rarely become over twelve inches tall and are usually much smaller; so never become too large to use as house plants.

Dracaena gracilis, see *Dracaena marginata*

Dracaena indivisa, see *Cordyline australis*

Dracaena marginata (*D. gracilis*), Red-Margined Dracaena (See Plate 10.)

At first glance one might mistake *Dracaena marginata* for one of the desert plants called Spanish Dagger, for it has great clusters of long blade-shaped leaves arising from the ends of each of its branches. These leaves are shiny green and edged with a reddish hue. They persist on the plants for a long while and are constantly being renewed by terminal growth. Older leaves which turn yellow may be removed with a slight tug. Unlike many cultivated Dracaenas, this type branches when young, but in an erratic and picturesque manner. It is a very tough and tolerant species which may eventually become several feet tall; so older plants are particularly suited for use in large rooms.

Dracaena sanderiana, Sander's Dracaena

Sander's Dracaena has been grown for many years because its gray-green, white-margined leaves are colorful and long lasting and because the species is tough and tolerant of house conditions. Young plants appear to be fresh rosettes of lovely foliage, but as the plants grow older, they develop slender canes topped by clusters of attractive leaves. Small plants of this Dracaena are often used in dish gardens because they are so durable.

CHAPTER 8

DIEFFENBACHIAS OR DUMB CANES

When Dieffenbachias were first discovered growing in the jungles of Central and South America, they were the cause of considerable disagreement among the botanists of the day. Some were sure that they were new species of Caladiums, while others contended that they were Arums. Eventually, through more thorough study, it was apparent that they were entirely different, and they were named in honor of Herr J. F. Dieffenbach, a German botanist and physican who was in charge of the gardens at the imperial palace of Schönbrunn in Vienna.

Dieffenbachias acquired their present name in 1830; thus they have been grown as house plants for a long while. During most of these years the only ones available were the various species direct from the jungle. As good as they were, even better types have been developed in the greenhouses of plantsmen around the world.

Dieffenbachias make fine foliage plants for our modern homes, not only because of their intrinsic beauty, but also because they enjoy the warm temperatures we maintain. In fact, it is very important that they stay warm and are not set in a spot where they could receive cold drafts.

Another requirement is that the site chosen for them should have considerable light, but not direct sun. Certain types will tolerate darker spots than others, and this will be noted below.

Unlike some plants, Dieffenbachias do not like to have constantly moist soil. A good rule is to water them thoroughly when the soil becomes moderately dry; then let the soil become nearly dry before giving them another drink.

Young Dieffenbachias are graceful plants with broadly oval leaves which clothe them fully. As they mature, their foliage is restricted to pendant clusters atop each curving stem, much in the manner of miniature Palm trees. If short plants are wanted instead of tall ones, the tips can be air-layered until roots form, then removed and potted. Also, stem sections, if laid partly covered in moist sand, will send out young plants which may be removed and potted individually. Dieffenbachias take a long while to reach the overgrown stage, however; so these operations are rarely done by the home gardener.

Repotting may become necessary as plants become larger. Many commercial growers use pure peat moss as a "soil." Others mix equal parts of peat moss and rich loam, or equal parts peat moss, loam, well rotted cow manure, and sand. The purpose is to provide the highly organic base in which Dieffenbachias thrive. To keep plants healthy, but not growing too rapidly, give them a mild feeding with a house plant fertilizer every two to three months.

You have probably noticed that the English name for Dieffenbachia is Dumb Cane. This is in allusion to the fact that chewing on a leaf or stem will cause numbness of the tongue and temporary speechlessness.

There are scores of different Dieffenbachias to be found as wild plants throughout the islands of the Caribbean and the adjacent lands of Central and South America. Most of them are very much alike in general aspect, differing chiefly in the coloration of their leaves. Of all of these, the four types most commonly sold in this country, selections which have proved their durability as house plants, are listed below.

Dieffenbachia amoena

This lovely species is very tolerant of poor light conditions and has earned its place as one of the finest of Dieffenbachias.

It has deep green leaves blotched with white along the lateral veins. It is native to Costa Rica and Colombia and is one of the largest of the types grown as house plants. Mature leaves may be as much as eighteen inches long. Several plants of *D. amoena* grown together in a large tub make a most impressive sight.

Dieffenbachia arvida, see *D. exotica*

x *Dieffenbachia bausei*

The over-all appearance of this hybrid Dieffenbachia is that its foliage is a pale and delicate green, but closer inspection will show that there are dark green as well as white spots scattered irregularly across the leaf surfaces, and many of the leaves are edged with a thin strip of dark green.

Dieffenbachia brasiliensis, see *Dieffenbachia picta*

Dieffenbachia exotica (*D. arvida*) (See Plate 14.)

The highly mottled foliage of this species has assured it of an honored place among the Dieffenbachias. It is not a large-growing type but has a compact habit and such intense coloration that the creamy-white spots on the leaves seem to cover more surface than the basic green background.

Dieffenbachia picta Rudolph Roehrs (See Plate 15.)

The species *D. picta* (*D. brasiliensis*), a native of Brazil, is given to many forms, but none of them is more appealing than the mutation called Rudolph Roehrs. In this plant the broad, arching leaves appear in several shades of green approaching chartreuse, the youngest leaves being of the lightest coloration. They are occasionally dotted with flecks of white and are bordered by narrow bands of dark green.

CHAPTER 9

TREE IVY
x (*Fatshedera lizei*)

Until a few years ago no such plant as Tree Ivy existed in the whole world. It was in 1910 that Lizé frères, nurserymen of Nantes, France, discovered an unusual seedling among their crop of Japanese Fatsias. As the plant matured, it became evident that it was a natural hybrid between English Ivy and Japanese Fatsia, two genera isolated in nature by the wide expanse of the continent of Eurasia, but brought together by accident in a French nursery. Its leaves were similar in shape to those of its English Ivy parent, but they were of huge dimensions, as much as eight to ten inches across, though commonly only half that size, and borne on an upright plant reminiscent of its Fatsia parent.

It is easy to understand how *Fatshedera* (See Plate 16.) got its botanical name; it is a simple combination of *Fatsia*, its Japanese parent, and *Hedera*, the botanical name for English Ivy. *Lizei*, of course, honors the brothers who were observant enough to spot this one plant among the thousands of other seedlings.

It was only natural that the Lizé brothers should win the grand prize at the flower show in Nantes in 1912, but it took many years for them to build up a quantity of plants. Each new plant had to be started from a cutting, for *Fatshedera* seeds are sterile, although the plants bear large clusters of tiny soft green flowers.

In 1926 the United States Department of Agriculture brought the first Tree Ivy plants to this country. Since that time their progeny have spread into flower shops and homes and even into gardens in mild sections of the country. During the course of the years a lovely green and white mutation appeared and was given the name *Fatshedera lizei variegata*.

Tree Ivies have certain unusual characteristics which have enabled them to compete against the other fine foliage plants already in commerce. For one thing, they can stand cold weather very well and are a good choice for planting close to an outside door where cold drafts are inevitable. They will tolerate temperatures as low as twenty-five degrees Fahrenheit without injury if they are not in active growth.

Another item very much in their favor is that they will stand sunny locations, as well as light shade. They do best in an evenly moist, but well-drained, organically rich soil. Professional growers often use a mixture made up of two parts peat moss and one part sandy loam, or one part peat moss, two parts leaf mold, and one part sand. Tree Ivies will remain in good health if fed every three months with a mild house plant fertilizer. Foliage care consists of washing the leaves occasionally with tepid water, or even wiping them with a damp cloth.

Tree Ivies last for years and hold their lower leaves well. The tips of new growth may be pinched out to foster branchiness, or the plants may be trained up a slab of bark, into which they will readily send aerial roots.

CHAPTER 10

PALMS FOR THAT TROPICAL TOUCH

Nearly all of us yearn for a pleasant land of Palms when wintry winds begin to blow. Many, indeed, take to southern climates for a while during the winter, but for considerably less money one may have Palms of his own indoors, though perhaps not large enough to lounge beneath. Some of the species listed below become large trees in their native lands, but as young plants they make interesting and long-lived house plants; others never become more than a few feet tall no matter how long they live. You will find that Palms are interesting foliage plants, well suited to house culture.

In general, Palms need but little care. They do best in a soil mixture composed of equal parts of rich loam, peat moss, and sharp sand and, when potted, should have this mixture firmed well about their roots. They do most of their growing during spring and early summer months and have little activity during the balance of the year. Soil beneath Palms should stay evenly moist at all times.

Most Palms do best in filtered light, and any exceptions will be noted below. They benefit by being placed outdoors under light shade during mild summer weather. There they should be watered freely, especially on the foliage to keep it clean and healthy. Feeding in the way of a mild general-purpose house plant fertilizer may be given once a month during the growing season, but not for the balance of the year.

While Palm foliage is distinctive and Palms are easily recognized as such by most persons, the species grown as house plants are divided into two broad groupings: those with fan-shaped leaves and those with feathery foliage. For your convenience, the divisions are separated below.

PALMS WITH FAN-SHAPED FOLIAGE

Chamaerops excelsa, see *Trachycarpus fortunei*

Chamaerops humilis, European Fan Palm

The European Fan Palm is a dwarf species native to the Mediterranean region. It sends out stiff fan-shaped leaves from clusters of brown fiber-covered stems. It will stand full sun or part shade.

Livistona chinensis, Chinese Fan Palm

Unlike the preceding species, this one has a solitary trunk and huge fan-shaped leaves from the edges of which hang down long slender fibrous strands. This is not a Palm for small rooms, but is very effective when given space to develop. It should have filtered light.

Rhapsis excelsa, Large Lady Palm; *R. humilis,* Slender Lady Palm

Both of these species are much alike except in size and have deep green fan-shaped leaves which arise from clusters of slender fiber-covered stems. Give Lady Palms light shade.

Trachycarpus fortunei (Chamaerops excelsa), Windmill Palm

The Windmill Palm is a commonly grown species especially good for cool locations. Its solitary hairy trunk has tough fan-shaped dark green leaves somewhat folded accordion-fashion. It should have abundant light, but not full sun.

PALMS WITH FEATHER-SHAPED FOLIAGE

Areca lutescens, see *Chrysalidocarpus lutescens*

Caryota (several species), Fishtail Palm

Fishtail Palms get their name from the fact that each seg-
ment of foliage on their long arching petioles is wedge-shaped
in the manner of a fish's tail. In a sense, too, the leaves look
somewhat like gigantic Maidenhair Ferns, and one has a feeling
that they belong to plant life of the Carboniferous Age. Give
Fishtail Palms protection from full sun.

Chamaedorea elegans bella (*Neanthe bella*), Parlor Palm (See
Plate 17.)

The Parlor Palm is undoubtedly the most common species
grown as a house plant in this country. It is an enchanting
dwarf type which grows in the jungle shade in the mystical
land of the Mayas in eastern Guatemala. If it is given a spot
where there is light, but no sunshine, it will last for years. Its
pinnate foliage arches gracefully from slender stems on plants
which rarely become over two feet tall under household conditions.

Chrysalidocarpus lutescens (*Areca lutescens*), Butterfly Palm

Mature plants of the Butterfly Palm may become huge
clumps of stems as much as twenty-five feet tall, clothed with
gracefully sweeping pinnate leaves, but as pot plants they are
much more tractable. Young specimens make fine bushy house
plants which do well if given a well-lighted spot sheltered from
the direct rays of the sun.

Cocos weddelliana, see *Syagrus weddelliana*

Howea belmoreana (*Kentia belmoreana*), Sentry Palm

This species has elegant long pinnate leaves of deepest green on single-trunked plants. It is grown commercially, but it is not as popular as its related species, *H. forsteriana*. It should have shelter from direct sun.

Howea forsteriana (*Kentia forsteriana*), Paradise Palm

It is this dark-foliaged Palm which is so often used by florists as decorations for weddings and other occasions. In commercial practice several plants are often set together in a tub so as to make a good showing of thick foliage. Paradise Palms do well as house plants. Give them filtered light.

Kentia, see *Howea*

Neanthe bella, see *Chamaedorea elegans bella*

Phoenix roebeleni, Miniature Date Palm

This attractive species is surely one of the nicest of Palms for indoor culture. Its dark green pinnate leaves are so long and graceful that they often form semicircles, even curving under a pot set upon a stand. It will last for many years as an interesting and satisfactory house plant. Give it light shade.

Syagrus weddelliana (*Cocos weddelliana*), Weddell Syagrus Palm

In the florist trade this Palm goes by the name of *Cocos weddelliana,* and for many years has been widely grown because of its dwarf stature and graceful, feathery yellow-green foliage. It should be given light shade.

CHAPTER 11

GET ACQUAINTED WITH NEPHTHYTIS

It's too bad that Nephthytis is such an odd name. To compound the confusion, the name Nephthytis is a misnomer, for the plants grown and sold in commerce under that name are really members of the genus *Syngonium*. The reason given for the switch is that someone thought that Nephthytis sounded more euphonious than Syngonium. As poor an excuse as that is, the fact remains that the plants we call Nephthytis come from the jungles of Central America and the islands of the Caribbean, while true Nephthytises are somewhat similar plants from the humid coastal areas of Liberia and Sierra Leone on the Atlantic coast of equatorial Africa. They are rarely grown in this country because they demand the sticky atmosphere of the tropics.

Nephthytises are outstanding in the extraordinary health they exhibit while growing under poor light conditions. Their habit of growth lies between that of creepers and climbers. They will gladly climb a bark-covered slab of wood, for example, but they are equally at home when denied a support, and under these conditions become graceful trailing plants which do not grow too rapidly.

The leaf shape of Nephthytises varies from ones of simple arrowhead design to others with three to five unequal-sized segments. Leaf color, however, is the important horticultural consideration of these interesting plants. Although some types have plain green leaves, most of the ones sold today are variously marked with areas of white, cream, yellow, silver, and various shades of green. The names of these selections are intriguing and often give hints as to the leaf color to be expected. Green Gold (See Plate 18.), Emerald Gem, Trileaf Wonder, Imperial White, Frost Queen, and Fantasy are commonly grown varieties.

The one requirement that Nephthytises ask is that the soil beneath them stay uniformly moist at all times. The soil mixture itself can be made of equal parts of peat moss, loam, and sand.

Do not be dissuaded from growing Nephthytises because of their unfamiliar name. You will find that they are among the easiest of the smaller foliage plants to grow and so satisfactory that you will soon be eager to heap upon them the superlatives they merit.

CHAPTER 12

CHOOSE PODOCARPUS FOR PERMANENCE

Botanists tell us that there are fifty-five species of Podocarpuses growing in tropical and subtropical regions of the world, ranging from the slopes of Mount Kenya in mid-Africa through the islands of Indonesia to Australia, South America, China, and Japan. Throughout their natural habitat Podocarpuses are valued as fine timber trees, but in this country we think of them as magnificent ornamental plants. In southern gardens Podocarpuses have long been known as Southern Yew, or even "Japanese Yew," but this name is apt to be misleading because it rightfully belongs to another closely related plant, *Taxus cuspidata.*

Even casual observers can see the natural kinship between Yews and Podocarpuses. In fact, the only apparent difference is that the Podocarpuses have much larger needles, often three to four inches long, while Yew foliage is usually less than one inch in length.

The Podocarpus most often grown as a house plant is the compact, dark-foliaged species known as *Podocarpus macrophylla maki* (See Plate 19.). There is a special reason why this type is unusual in its family, and why it makes a long-lasting house plant of exceptional beauty. Unlike its timber-bearing relatives, this species is of a dense, slow-growing nature. It can be happy for years in a large flowerpot or tub without outgrowing its bounds. As a matter of fact, one can easily limit its growth by pruning if it should become larger than desired.

Another fine feature of Podocarpuses is that they will thrive under cool conditions. Many foliage plants must have tropical warmth in order to survive, but Podocarpuses will do beautifully in cold spots as well as warm ones.

Podocarpuses are happy under wide ranges of light conditions. They will stand full sunshine or quite deep shadows. About the only noticeable difference in a shady spot is that the leaves are of a deeper green hue and that growth is slower than in a sunnier location.

The soil requirements of Podocarpuses are very simple. A mixture of equal parts of loam, peat moss, and sand will satisfy their needs. It should be kept evenly moist at all times, but not saturated. It is important to remember that the soil should never be allowed to become dry. Feed plants twice a year with a mild house plant fertilizer.

Even small Podocarpuses often blossom and set fruit. The greenish female flowers are inconspicuous, but the golden-yellow male catkins are very showy. The name Podocarpus, from the Greek *podos*, a foot, and *karpos*, a fruit, alludes to its strange edible two-parted fruit. Each fruit consists of a large pink fleshy berrylike section connected by a tiny stem to another greenish berry which contains the seed itself.

It should be mentioned that since Podocarpuses are coniferous evergreens, they, like all others, lose their oldest needles each year, but they are more than replaced by the new ones which appear before the older ones fall.

It is truly difficult to find anything wrong with Podocarpuses as house plants. Try them yourself and you will agree. They are lovely both in over-all appearance and under close inspection; they will last for years with a minimum of attention, and they need not grow too large because pruning can limit their size. Best of all, their soft dark green needles blend with any décor.

CHAPTER 13

THE JAPANESE PITTOSPORUM

Until recent years the Japanese Pittosporum, *Pittosporum tobira*, was known almost exclusively as an evergreen garden shrub in mild sections of the country, but it is now being offered as a house plant as well. Its sturdy, tongue-shaped leaves are rich green on the original species and milky green, tipped with white markings on the plant known as *P. tobira variegata* (See Plate 20.). Both are excellent, compact-growing shrubs of globular configuration. They prefer a sunny spot, but will do quite well under light shade as well. In addition to their attractive foliage, these species have delightfully fragrant terminal clusters of creamy white flowers with much the scent of Orange blossoms. Flowers are not always borne on young plants, but sunshiny locations will help to induce blossoming.

Pittosporums are particularly useful as foliage plants in the home because relatively few other types will stand full sun, nor will many others tolerate cool temperatures. If need be, Pittosporums may be kept barely above freezing during their dormant season, so are natural choices for entrance plantings which may be subject to cold drafts as doors are opened and closed.

A simple soil mixture composed of equal parts of loam, peat moss, and sand will suit Pittosporums. It should be given a thorough soaking, then allowed to become slightly dry before more water is applied. Feeding should be limited to twice a year with any house plant fertilizer. This will maintain healthy foliage without encouraging excessive growth. Under outdoor culture Pittosporums may become four to five feet or more tall and equally as broad, but pot-grown plants are of more limited size and may be kept as small as necessary by pruning at any time.

CHAPTER 14

SPATHIPHYLLUMS COMBINE FOLIAGE AND FLOWERS

Spathiphyllums are members of the Arum family, whose most familiar representatives are Philodendrons. Like their rugged cousins, Spathiphyllums are able to endure poorly lighted spots month after month and continue to be perfectly happy. What is more, it is under these conditions that Spathiphyllums produce, usually during summer and fall, their lovely crops of long-lasting, subtly scented, snowy white flowers which look much like those of Calla-Lilies.

Botanists claim to have discovered twenty-seven species of Spathiphyllums in the jungles of South America and Malaysia, but strangely enough, the ones grown commercially are not among them. The most common one grown is S. *clevelandii* (See Plate 21.), which is believed to have originated as a chance hybrid in a New Jersey greenhouse late in the nineteenth century. When Grover Cleveland became President in 1885, it was named in his honor. Another variety, Mauna Loa, was hybridized in recent years in a Los Angeles greenhouse and has larger flowers than those of S. *clevelandii*, and they are produced throughout the year. Other selections are occasionally found, but these are the two most frequently grown as house plants.

One of the nice things about Spathiphyllums is that they never become too large for their surroundings. They are not climbers, but send out all of their long, narrow, glistening dark green leaves from the bases of the plants. When plants become too crowded, it is a simple matter to divide the clumps and repot the plants into a soil mixture composed of equal parts of sand, peat moss, leaf mold, and rich loam. Spathiphyllums like a humusy soil to such an extent that many florists grow them in pure peat moss, or in a half-and-half mixture of peat moss and sand. The soil should stay quite moist at all times. Feeding may be in the form of any mild house plant fertilizer applied every two to three months.

Spathiphyllums are happiest when grown in a warm and humid spot out of the sun. They enjoy temperatures of seventy to eighty degrees Fahrenheit and need little care except an occasional cleaning of their beautiful leaves by wiping them with a damp cloth.

You will find that Spathiphyllums will continue to send out lovely flowers from their crowns of rich green foliage in dimly lighted spots which would discourage most house plants. Despite their strange-sounding name, you will like Spathiphyllums.

CHAPTER 15

THE NORFOLK ISLAND PINE
(*Araucaria*)

Few plants illustrate the fickleness of tastes in horticulture more vividly than does the Norfolk Island Pine. In publication after publication this coniferous evergreen from the southern hemisphere is being hailed as a "new" house plant of sterling qualities. The last part is surely true, for few house plants are as enduring and as graceful, but it is hardly correct to consider it new to indoor gardening. A garden writer at the beginning of the twentieth century said, "Araucarias are probably the most prized pot evergreens in cultivation. They are much used in house decoration, particularly at Christmastime, as they are not only attractive, but will stand much hard usage." World wars have come and gone since that time, and Norfolk Island Pines practically disappeared from commerce, but now they are back with a flourish to lend their gracefulness to our modern homes as they did for those belonging to our grandmothers.

About a dozen species of Araucarias are to be found in such out-of-the-way spots as southern Chile, Patagonia, Australia, New Caledonia, New Guinea, and Norfolk Island, a remote speck of land lying between New Caledonia and Australia. It is the species *A. excelsa* (See Plate 30.) from Norfolk Island, that is the best for pot culture. Its soft green needles lie close to tiered, horizontally held branches in typical Pine-tree shape.

It is amazing to learn that mature trees on Norfolk Island become over two hundred feet tall and up to ten feet in diameter, for as house plants their growth is extremely slow and sedate. It has been found in experimental work that growth rates of

Norfolk Island Pines can range from two and one half inches per year to over three feet per year, depending upon the supply of food and moisture available. Unless one is eager to have a large tree with widely spaced branches, it is best not to give Araucarias too much food. As a matter of fact, two or three light feedings of a houseplant fertilizer each year will be ample for their needs.

A soil mixture made up of equal parts of loam, peat moss, and sand will serve Araucarias well. It should be kept evenly moist at all times.

Norfolk Island Pines will stand full sunshine except during the hottest months of the year, when they should be given some protection. They are also remarkably tolerant of dim light, too, and if not fed too often, or kept too wet, will do beautifully for years under rather poor light conditions. The ability to survive and retain beauty under adverse situations is one definite reason why Norfolk Island Pines are now enjoying such an amazing comeback.

A word should be said about the reproduction of Norfolk Island Pines because the growth habit, as well as growth rate, is dependent upon the method of propagation, and this in turn has a decided effect upon the cost of the plants. The easiest method of production is to grow the plants from seeds. Such young trees grow relatively quickly and are the ones most commonly seen in commerce today. It is a strange but true fact that plants grown from erect terminal cuttings produce slower growing, more compact specimens. These plants are much more costly, not only because they grow more slowly, but because only a limited number of terminal cuttings can be produced from a "mother" plant. As a matter of fact, only one terminal cutting can be produced the first time because only the central trunk has an upright terminal shoot. After the first cutting is taken, the plant will, in time, send out three or four axillary shoots, each of which will be erect in habit. None of the side branches will produce upright-growing trees, but only lopsided specimens of no commercial value. Thus cutting production is very limited and extremely costly as compared to seedlings.

The name "Monkey Puzzle Tree" is sometimes applied to *A. excelsa*, but it more correctly belongs to the allied species *A. imbricata* from Chile, a spiny-leafed form which is grown outdoors in mild areas of this country.

CHAPTER 16

FERNS AS HOUSE PLANTS

It is interesting from the point of view of a flower lover to note the resurgence of attention that Ferns are receiving nowadays. Many years ago every home had at least one beautiful specimen, usually a form of Boston Fern, in its parlor. Older readers will recall the tall wicker stands on which plants stood so that their fronds could cascade gracefully on every side. About a generation ago the vogue began a gradual decline, but now there is a healthy upsurge of curiosity about these long-neglected plants. Indoor gardeners are amazed to see the diversity of foliage among the Ferns and are not a little chagrined to learn that these same varieties of plants were their grandmothers' favorites.

One of the reasons that Ferns did well during Victorian days was that lack of central heating resulted in cooler rooms with higher relative humidity. Today, atmospheric moisture continues to be the most decisive factor in Fern culture. Those who live in humid areas such as the Northwest can grow Ferns with ease, but others with dry mid-continent climates find the task exceedingly difficult. No matter how dry the climate, however, one may grow Ferns with ease in terrariums and indoor greenhouses, subjects discussed in Chapter 26. Many of the low-growing types described below make ideal terrarium subjects.

Ferns do well when grown on trays of moist sand, pebbles, sawdust, peat moss, or any other material from which water can gradually evaporate into the air around the plants. For the same reason several plants set close together do better than one standing alone.

In addition to moist air, Ferns must have a moist, humusy soil in which to grow. Although there are aquatic Ferns, the ones grown as house plants like a combination of high moisture content and good drainage. A suitable soil mixture is one composed of equal parts of loam, sand, peat moss, and leaf mold, plus a dusting of bone meal. It should be kept moist, but pots should not stand in water. The above soil mixture will suit all Ferns listed in this section unless noted otherwise.

It is common knowledge that Ferns grow in shady places. Thus it is not surprising that we find some very satisfactory house plants among them, since low light levels in homes are usually responsible for poor growth of most ordinary house plants. All Ferns do best in filtered light, but some will withstand poorer conditions than others; these will be noted below. While Ferns like shady places, there is a limit to the amount of shade they can endure. For that reason, they, like other house plants, respond well to supplementary illumination.

In greenhouses where fast plant growth is essential to profit, it is common practice to feed Ferns about once every three months. Under the reduced light levels of house culture feeding should be restricted to six-month intervals, and then at very dilute solutions. Ferns do not need much fertilizer at any time, and usually the soil in which they are received from a florist will suffice for a long while.

One of the important things to remember about Ferns is that their fronds are delicate, and great care should be taken so that they are placed in such a location so that they will not be brushed against in the house. Once a frond tip has been injured, it will turn brown, and the natural grace of the plant will have been lessened.

Although botanists recognize over six thousand species of Ferns which range in size from creeping threadlike plants to trees that become eighty feet tall, the following list is, nevertheless, very representative of the family as a whole. All of them are in commerce, but, as will be noted below, they vary somewhat in their ability to thrive under household conditions.

Adiantum, Maidenhair Fern

The delicate-foliaged Maidenhair Ferns are among the most admired of all, but they are not easy to grow as house plants, except in areas where there is an abundance of natural atmospheric moisture. The soil should stay moist at all times, but the plants should not sit in water. Except in humid climates, Maidenhair Ferns are best grown in shady conservatories or in terrariums. The smaller species make very attractive house plants where they can be grown successfully. The two species responsible for most of the Maidenhair Ferns grown today are *A. cuneatum* from Brazil and *A. tenerum* from the West Indies and southern Mexico. They are to be found in innumerable varieties, two of the better ones being *A. cuneatum* Goldelse and *A. tenerum wrightii.* Tropical species of Maidenhair Ferns are often grown in gardens in mild climates, and the native *A. pedatum* grows wild as far north as Alaska.

Aspidium, see *Polystichum*

Asplenium, Spleenwort

Two tropical species of *Asplenium* are graceful and unusual Ferns commonly available from florists and greenhouses. The one most often seen is the Bird's Nest Fern, *A. nidus,* whose fronds appear decidedly unlike those of most Ferns. Instead of being divided into feathery sections, they are long and tonguelike in appearance and arise from a central crown of black "hairs." It is this crown, nestling among the fronds, which reminds a viewer of a bird's nest. The other remarkable species is *A. bulbiferum,* known as Mother Spleenwort or Mother Fern because it produces bulbils upon its finely cut foliage which put forth tiny plants while still attached to the parent leaves. The Bird's Nest Fern is native in the Far East from Japan and India

1. The singular charm of a specimen plant at a window. Here illustrated is the rhizomatous Begonia known as "Cleopatra" or "Maphil."

2. The Golden Pothos, *Scindapsus aureus,* is especially suited for culture as a trailing plant.

5. An entrance to home conservatory planted to shade-loving Begonias, *Pteris* or Table Ferns, and *Dieffenbachia picta* Rudolph Roehrs.

4. The most common of house plants, the Heartleaf Philodendron, can add a new dimension of delight to indoor gardening.

5. The graceful beauty of Maidenhair Ferns continues to enchant each new generation of flower lovers.

6. Supplementary artificial light assures the health of this exotic *Monstera deliciosa*.

7. A collection of foliage plants makes this corner of a conservatory a peaceful oasis in a busy household. Among the plants illustrated are Parlor Palm, Neph-thytis, Pothos, Artillery Plant, Bird-of-Paradise, Ferns, and several types of Begonias.

8. A stairway planting of several easy-to-grow foliage plants, including Heart-leaf Philodendron, Sansevieria, and Sander's Dracaena.

southward through the islands to Australia. The Mother Fern grows wild from New Zealand and Australia northward through most of the Malay Peninsula.

Cibotium, Cibotium Fern

Cibotium Ferns are the ones which are so often used by florists in wedding decorations, being placed on tall stands so that their golden-green fronds, which spread to a diameter of five to eight feet, may be seen to best advantage. Generally speaking, these plants are too large for most homes, but a single plant in a conservatory gives a sense of the tropics difficult to achieve in any other way. The Cibotium species most commonly seen is *C. schiedei,* called simply Cibotium Fern, or more correctly Mexican Cibotium Fern. It is sometimes called Mexican Tree Fern because it becomes fifteen feet tall in its native mountainous habitat in Mexico. Tip sections of two species of Hawaiian Tree Ferns, *C. chamissoi* and *C. menziesii,* are sometimes sold in this country. They will live for a long while in a vase of water and send forth lovely soft green fronds.

Cyathea, Tree Fern

One of the most interesting of the Tree Ferns is the species *Cyathea arborea,* which was introduced into England from the West Indies by Admiral (formerly Captain) Bligh in 1793. It grows to be fifty feet tall on the Caribbean Islands, but specimens five to six feet tall are more commonly seen in conservatories in this country. The soil beneath these plants should be kept moist at all times.

Cyrtomium, Holly Fern

One of the easiest of the Ferns to grow as a house plant is the Holly Fern, known as *Cyrtomium falcatum rochefordianum,* a variety selected for its wide, dark green, serrated leaflets which look amazingly like Holly foliage. This plant will stand very poor light conditions. Most house plant specimens grow from ten to eighteen inches tall.

Davallia, Rabbit's Foot Fern

The most common *Davallia* used as a house plant is the species *D. fejeensis,* the Rabbit's Foot Fern, a native of the Fiji Islands. It, as well as other *Davallia* species, has hairy, creeping, above-ground rootstalks which account for its common name. It does very well as a house plant and should have a shady location and be kept moist.

Nephrolepis, Sword Fern

It is the Sword Fern, in one of its countless varieties, which is the Fern most commonly grown as a house plant. Although the original species has ordinary pinnate fronds, some of its mutations have foliage most extraordinarily divided and crisped. It is interesting to note that occasionally these varieties revert by putting forth a frond or two with the plain foliage of the original species.

Almost all of the varieties of Sword Fern are derived from *Nephrolepis exaltata,* a species which grows from Florida to southern South America, as well as in Africa, southern Asia, Australia, and the islands of the South Pacific. Servicemen who served in the island-hopping campaigns of World War II can recall carpets of Sword Ferns underlying the groves of Coconut Palms.

The most common variety of Sword Fern is called the Boston Fern. This incongruous name, in the light of the nativity of the species, came into being about the turn of the century when a florist in Cambridge, Massachusetts found an unusual and different Fern in a shipment from a wholesaler. Eventually it was sent to a botanist at Kew Gardens in London for identification. He declared it to be a distinct form and suggested the name Boston Fern. Within a few years the original Boston Fern began to send forth amazing mutations, and its simple pinnate fronds became, in its progeny, increasingly subdivided into smaller and smaller thickly set segments. Thus it becomes almost a personal choice when picking the better types of Boston Ferns as house plants. Nevertheless, the following are typical varieties that are available commercially.

Nephrolepis exaltata bostoniensis, Boston Fern

This selection has long pendant fronds and is one of the easiest to grow, but because of its size, it has been largely superseded by its dwarf form.

Nephrolepis exaltata bostoniensis compacta, Dwarf Boston Fern

This variety, grown for many years, has the simple pinnate leaves of the original species, but is small enough and tolerant enough to make a good house plant for most homes.

Nephrolepis exaltata Colorado

The Colorado Sword Fern is a larger growing type than some, with rather stiff, erect fronds which eventually droop as they mature.

Nephrolepis exaltata Fluffy Ruffles (See Plate 22.)

The person who named this variety chose wisely both from the descriptive and commercial point of view. It is a dwarf type, rarely over twelve inches tall, and has lively green, leathery, intricately divided fronds of exceptional beauty.

Nephrolepis exaltata Trevillian

The fronds of this lovely type are so subdivided into tiny segments that they look more oval than flat in cross section. The plants are medium-sized growers among the Sword Ferns, reaching eighteen inches tall, and are good house plants.

Nephrolepis exaltata Verona

Verona is not a new variety, but it is a good one under house conditions. Its fronds are lacelike in appearance, and the plants are of reasonably compact growth, both attributes which have contributed to its continued popularity.

Platycerium bifurcatum, Staghorn Fern

Unless you have a warm and shady conservatory, you probably will not have suitable conditions for growing the well-named Staghorn Fern. Its foliage consists of two parts, one of which flows around its support, often a piece of bark-covered wood, in a smooth, tight-fitting mantle of gray green. It is from this base that the "horns" spring forth. They are flat, drooping fronds variously divided in the manner of antlers. This species is native to certain of the South Pacific islands from New Caledonia northward through New Guinea.

Polypodium aureum mandaianum, Manda's Hare's Foot Fern

Several species of *Polypodium* Ferns grow throughout the world, but the only one chosen for this list is the selected form noted above. It grows in somewhat the same way as do species of *Davallia,* but the above-ground rootstalks are larger. Its blue-green fronds are wavy and delicately cut along the margins.

Polystichum tsus-simense (Aspidium tsus-simense), Tsussima
Holly Fern

This low-growing Fern with the long name is native to the
Tsu Islands in the Korea Strait, between Japan and the main-
land. It is a good Fern for house culture because it is relatively
small and can do with lower humidity than some species, provided the soil is kept moist. Plants ultimately become two feet
tall, but are more apt to be only half that height. Fronds are
pale to medium green and are divided into small pointed segments.

Pteris, Table Fern

Table Ferns get their name from the fact that they are often
used as table decorations, since their dwarf nature and ease of
culture makes them popular house Ferns. Three main species
are usually found, *cretica, ensiformis,* and *multifida,* but they
are further subdivided into any number of varieties whose foliage is often marked with silver or white and various shades of
green. There is every imaginable leaf form to be found among
Table Ferns. They like to be kept moist and in a shady spot.
Since many types are only six to eight inches tall at maturity,
Table Ferns are ideal as subjects for terrariums.

CHAPTER 17

THE MAGNIFICENT MONSTERA OR SWISS CHEESE PLANT
(Monstera deliciosa)

Of all the foliage plants grown in homes, Monsteras (See Plate 23.) draw the most expressions of awe and amazement from newcomers to indoor gardening. It is hard to conceive of a plant whose leaves are normally perforated in such an improbable manner. Botanists believe that this is an adaptation of nature to allow the leaves to survive the fierce winds of tropical hurricanes.

The name *Monstera* is an allusion to the serpentine stems of wild jungle specimens in Mexico which range from tree to tree trailing huge snakelike aerial roots. Its given name of *deliciosa* is in recognition of the fact that the fruit of this vine is delectable. It is shaped like large pine cones, and its flavor savors of both Banana and Pineapple. Plants rarely bear fruit under home conditions because they do not attain sufficient size.

It is interesting to note that Monsteras are known by different names, depending upon whether the plants are seedlings, with juvenile, less perforated leaves, or older plants with mature foliage. The seedlings are sold as *Philodendron pertusum,* but they really are young plants of *Monstera deliciosa.* Sometimes they are given the names of Cutleaf or Splitleaf Philodendrons, but they are not truly Philodendrons. In the tropics where Monsteras are grown for both fruit and ornament, they are called Cerimans, but in florist circles the botanical name of *Monstera* and the common name Swiss Cheese Plant are more frequently given.

Monsteras are tough and tolerant foliage plants which grow

slowly and live for many years as attractive house plants. They will survive temperatures nearly to freezing, but they will not make active growth until it becomes sixty-five degrees Fahrenheit or more. Ideally, they should have the humid warmth of the jungle, but they do beautifully in the drier air of our homes. They should have a well-lighted location, but no direct sunlight.

It is not necessary to feed Monsteras more than twice a year unless one wishes them to grow rapidly. Use a dilute house plant fertilizer in early spring and again in midsummer. The pot in which your Monstera comes from the florist should be sufficient for its needs for a year or more; then it can be given a larger one and repotted in soil similar to that recommended for Philodendrons. Soil for Monsteras should stay barely moist at all times.

Monsteras are often used as background plants for advertisement photographs with tropical settings because of the photogenic qualities of their marvelously perforated and pinnated leaves. Let Monsteras bring a bit of the tropics into your home.

CHAPTER 18

THE AGLAONEMA FAMILY

An up-to-date list of Aglaonemas might be cited as an example of the work being done by plant hunters in bringing into cultivation the new wealth of tropical plants which do so well in our homes. As recently as 1941 the authoritative *Hortus Second* listed nine species and varieties; in contrast, *Exotica 3*, published in 1963, describes twenty-seven Aglaonemas. Such an increase is indicative of the high regard in which the whole family is held by growers of house plants.

It would be difficult to find a plant of any kind which is able to live so happily with such little light as Aglaonemas. This one fact ought to endear them to housewives, for every home has at least one spot where a plant is needed, but light is lacking. Aglaonemas want a shady place with 50 to 500 foot-candles of light for a normal day length, compared with the 4000 to 8000 foot-candles required by most flowering plants. It should be remembered that Aglaonemas are from the tropics and need to be kept in a warm location (65 to 85° Fahrenheit).

As house plants, the various types of Aglaonemas vary from less than one foot to a bit more than two feet in height. Their compact growth habit and their clear green or mottled foliage has won them a lasting place among the better "green plants."

Aglaonemas occasionally blossom in the home, and when they do, they demonstrate their kinship to Calla-Lilies. Their greenish-white flowers are not showy, but they are followed by clusters of bright red or yellow beanlike fruit.

After a long period of time Aglaonemas lose some of their

lower and older leaves. This day can be delayed by feeding the plants with a very dilute house plant fertilizer about three times each year. New plants may be had by rooting tip cuttings in sand, then potting them up in a humusy soil mixture. Keep the soil beneath Aglaonemas barely moist at all times.

Aglaonemas have no common English names except for *A. modestum* and *A. simplex*, both of which are sold under the name Chinese Evergreen. The following species are the ones most widely available from flower shops and greenhouses. Any of them will do well in your home.

Aglaonema commutatum (*Schismatoglottis commutatum*)

This lovely Aglaonema is unique in that it rarely grows more than one foot tall, thus presents a compact picture of long-lasting beauty. Its lance-shaped leaves, roughly five inches long and two inches wide at their greatest dimensions, are a deep glistening green, mottled with silver-gray markings along each side of the lateral veins of each leaf. Since it is native to the densely shaded jungle floor of the Philippines, it is little wonder that it does so well in the dimly lighted interiors of our homes.

Aglaonema costatum

It might be easy to mistake this dwarf-growing Aglaonema for a type of Dieffenbachia, since its dark green leaves are dotted with white spots and have a streak of white down the midrib of each leaf.

Aglaonema modestum (*A. sinensis*), Chinese Evergreen

Flower shops have long sold plants of *A. modestum* as bare-rooted specimens to be grown in water. Of course, they will grow in soil also and be somewhat longer lived. Their large leaves are dark green, somewhat leathery, and very gracefully arranged along slender stalks.

Aglaonema pseudo-bracteatum, Variegated Chinese Evergreen (See Plate 24.)

This colorful Aglaonema with its large, pointed leaves, generously mottled with white and creamy yellow, is one of the most spectacular of the recent introductions. Plants may become two feet tall, but are usually somewhat smaller. This is a very desirable type and surely ought to be in any collection of indoor foliage plants.

Aglaonema roebelinii (Schismatoglottis roebelinii)

You may find this robust plant listed under either of the above names. It is much larger in all its parts than other cultivated Aglaonemas and has leaves which may be ten inches long and half as wide. They are a soft green in color and are boldly splashed with markings of gray on the upper surfaces. Since this plant becomes nearly three feet tall under ordinary conditions, it is a good subject for large tub plantings in areas of limited lighting.

Aglaonema simplex, Chinese Evergreen

This plant is very similar to *A. modestum,* but has somewhat narrower leaves. Bare-rooted plants will live in water for extended periods of time, especially if a few pieces of charcoal are placed in the water.

Aglaonema sinensis, see *Aglaonema modestum*

Aglaonema treubi

The long narrow leaves of *A. treubi* are blotched with gray green on their upper surfaces and are borne on rather dwarf plants which are usually under twelve inches in height. This is a fine species to grow in a spot where space is limited.

CHAPTER 19

THE COLORFUL CROTONS
(*Codiaeum*)

Sun-loving foliage plants are in the minority because most of the ones which do so well in our homes come from the shaded floors of tropical jungles. Crotons, however, revel in sunshine and are welcome brightly colored additions to the indoor world of house plants. Croton foliage comes in a bizarre assortment of colors. Combinations of yellow, green, and red are most common, but among the hundreds of variations of the species *Codiaeum variegatum pictum* one may find plants whose leaves exhibit shades of copper, purple, bronze, brown, pink, and orange, as well as white. A unique feature of Crotons is that leaves of many colors may be found on the same plant. Usually leaves which develop in sunshine are more highly colored than those which grow in partial shade.

All Croton leaves are thick, smooth, glossy, and of a leathery texture, but here the similarity ends. Not only are their colors exotic, but their shapes defy description. Some leaves are broad and have smooth edges; others are scalloped and lobed; certain ones have narrow foliage, and a few have leaves so twisted that they look like kaleidoscopic corkscrews.

It is often helpful in learning about the cultural requirements of plants to know something about the climate of the part of the world in which the plants are native. Crotons are indigenous to the humid tropics of the Malayan Peninsula and the islands of the South Pacific. It is an area in which there is daily rainfall throughout much of the year; thus the amount of moisture in the atmosphere is high. This factor is important in considering Crotons as house plants, but it is not nearly as critical as that of changing temperatures. Day and night temperatures rarely fluctuate more than a few degrees in their native environment, and the plants have become accustomed to this. Crotons resent rapid changes in temperature, and this has probably been the chief reason why some indoor gardeners have been unable to grow them successfully. You must not set Crotons in a cold draft, for sudden drops in temperature will result in nearly as sudden dropping of leaves. Otherwise, the tropical temperatures of our centrally heated homes provide an ideal climate for Crotons.

Crotons grow best in an evenly moist soil mixture composed of equal parts of rich loam, peat moss, sand, and leaf mold, although nearly any highly organic soil will meet their needs. Plants should be fed sparingly every three months from early spring until midsummer, but not for the balance of the year.

Red spider mites and mealy bugs have an affinity for Crotons. These can be controlled with insecticides, but an equally practical household method is to spray the foliage forceably with tepid water every week or so. These baths will keep the foliage dust free and gleaming and will wash away small-insect populations before they become troublesome.

In mild climates Crotons are grown as garden shrubs as well as pot plants. Gardeners in northern areas may use them as colorful bedding plants during the summer months.

CHAPTER 20

CITRUS TREES AS HOUSE PLANTS

Most of the plants discussed in this book are grown only for their lovely foliage, but the Citrus family combines glossy, deep green leaves with exquisitely fragrant white blossoms, which are followed by beautiful edible fruit. What is also important from the point of view of the gardener is that these plants are sun lovers. Most "green plants" must be given at least light shade in order to do well, but Citrus plants like the full sun, although they will tolerate filtered light if bright sunshine is not available.

There are several types of Oranges, Lemons, and Kumquats which may be grown as house plants. All do well in a soil mixture composed of equal parts of loam, peat moss, and sand. They grow quite rapidly when young, but much more slowly when old, thereby staying within bounds for many years. Size can always be reduced by pruning in the very early spring before the advent of new growth. In watering Citrus trees, give them a thorough soaking; then let them become quite dry before adding more moisture. Feed them with a regular house plant fertilizer about three times each year, once in the early spring, again in late spring or early summer, and finally in late summer or early fall. Do not feed them during winter when the plants are not in active growth.

It should be said that Citrus trees do best in cool locations where night temperatures range from fifty to sixty degrees Fahrenheit. Daytime readings can be considerably higher. Although they might enjoy more humid conditions than most homes allow, they nevertheless are very tolerant of dry air provided they receive regular moisture at their roots.

During the warm months of the year Citrus trees which have been grown as house plants may be set outdoors in a lightly shaded spot. Full sun might injure the foliage, which is accustomed to the protection of indoor living. It is beneficial to syringe the foliage from time to time to keep it clean and wash away harmful insects.

In order to have fruit, Citrus blossoms must be fertilized. If the plants are outdoors when they blossom, bees will gladly do the job. Indoors one may easily transfer pollen from flower to flower with a soft brush. Pollen from the same plant or from any other Citrus plant may be used, since the species hybridize freely. The resultant fruit will be typical of the parent tree, but seedlings would show hybrid origin. Citrus fruit clings to trees for many months after becoming ripe; so one often has blossoms as well as fruit on the trees at the same time.

It is a very common practice for persons to grow seedlings of Oranges or Grapefruit. Often these become quite sizable and develop vicious thorns, but fail to blossom or set fruit. It is remotely possible to get a satisfactory Orange or Grapefruit tree suitable for growing outdoors in warm climates, but it is next to impossible to grow a suitable house plant from such beginnings. Try one of the following types, however, and you will be very pleased with the results.

x *Citrus limonia meyeri,* Meyer Lemon

The Meyer Lemon is often grown as a home-garden variety in warm climates, but it also makes a very attractive small tree for house culture. The fruit is similar to that which we buy for home use.

x *Citrus limonia ponderosa,* Ponderosa Lemon

Perhaps you already are growing a Ponderosa Lemon tree, or have a friend who grows one. At any rate, they do very well in the house and bear huge Lemons, each big enough to make several delicious pies. Although mature trees may become eight to ten feet tall, they may easily be kept three to four feet in height and will bear a continuing crop of fruit. When your Ponderosa Lemon tree bears its first fruit, have a dinner party with you-know-what for dessert.

Citrus mitis, Calamondin or Panama Orange (See Plate 26.)

The Calamondin Orange is the most popular house plant of all the Citrus species because it is dwarf in stature and has prolific crops of fragrant blossoms and deep orange-yellow fruit set among tiny glossy leaves. Most plants sold by florists range from twelve to eighteen inches tall, and may be kept at this height for years by light pruning each spring. Its fruit is delicious, as well as ornamental, and has a flavor somewhere between that of an ordinary Orange and a Lime and makes a spicy addition to a beverage.

Citrus otaitense, see *Citrus taitensis*

Citrus sinensis, Sweet Orange

Perhaps you have never thought of growing ordinary Orange Trees in your house, but they will do quite well in a cool, brightly lighted spot. Keep them within bounds by annual pruning. My three-foot tree bore a baker's dozen of full-sized delicious fruit last season. This type of tree is not often offered by local florists, who have little call for them, but perhaps you can bring one home from a winter vacation trip to an Orange-growing area of the country. Sweet Oranges, as well as most other Citrus species, are native to southern China.

Citrus taitensis (*C. otaitense*), Otaheite Orange

The Otaheite Orange has been grown for many years as an ornamental plant. Its fruit is tart and golden in color and about half the size of ordinary Oranges. The tree is dwarf in nature and makes an excellent subject for a large pot or tub in which it can be kept for a number of years.

Fortunella hindsii, Dwarf Kumquat

Kumquats are among the more dwarf-growing of the Citrus relatives and make interesting pot plants. This species bears reddish-orange fruit less than one inch in diameter. Keep the soil beneath Kumquats evenly moist at all times.

Fortunella margarita, Nagami Kumquat

This species bears oval golden-orange fruit about one and one half inches long. It is delicious and may be eaten raw or made into preserves.

CHAPTER 21

SMALL VINES FOR INDOOR GARDENING

Elsewhere in this book you will find cultural suggestions for Climbing Philodendrons and other large plants, but here, for the sake of convenience, are gathered together the few species of small-growing vines that are excellent foliage plants. It should be known that, while these plants are climbers by nature, many of them are to be seen at their best when grown as hanging-basket or wall-bracket plants. Either way you grow them will suit the plants, as well as add a new dimension of interest to indoor gardening.

Asparagus plumosus, Asparagus-Fern

Do you have special memories connected with certain plants? One of the most vivid I can recall is that a beautiful Asparagus-Fern used to grow on the stair landing of my aunt's and uncle's home in Massachusetts. As I remember it, the plant was close to a window that looked out onto a covered porch. Such a site was a good one, for there was an abundance of light, but no direct sun.

Asparagus-Ferns usually send out several nonclimbing growths before they are strong enough to climb. Once they are established, they will quickly ascend a piece of twine, or they may be trained around a small trellis. Remember that in addition to their filmy green sprays of foliage, they also develop rather formidable thorns.

A basic soil mixture of equal parts of loam, peat moss, and

sand will suit them very well; it should be kept moist, but not wet, for best growth.

Asparagus sprengeri, see Chapter 23, Minor Foliage Plants

Bowiea volubilis (*Schizobasopsis*), Climbing Onion

It may seem like a joke to you that this queer little plant should be included among the vines for house culture. Its weird growth habits are so unlike that of other plants, however, that it deserves a place, if only for its conversation-inducing qualities.

The Climbing Onion, a native of South Africa, starts as a greenish-yellow bulb and sends forth in late fall a single stem of pale green growth that looks at first much like a thin spear of Asparagus. It grows at an astonishing rate to a height of three to five feet, twining about any support available. Its most astonishing feature is that it has no leaves, but its green stems, which branch abundantly, serve the same purpose as leaves. At the tips of this soft growth are borne tiny greenish-yellow flowers in late winter and spring. During the growth period the bulb should have abundant moisture, but after flowering, it will die back to the bulb, which should be stored in a dry place from May until October. Certainly this is not a plant for year-round effect, but it is just different enough to have a lot of admirers. Give it a spot with good light; it can even grow in full sun in any ordinary soil if kept reasonably cool.

Cissus (several varieties), Treebine

Some of the very best of the small indoor vines are to be found in the *Cissus* family. The various species offer a diversity of leaf forms, and, in addition, though they are vines, they respond to a minimum of training to serve as bushy specimens, or as hanging-basket and wall-planter subjects because the cascading stems have such inherent grace. They cling to supports by tendrils, which indicate their close relationship to Grape vines.

Small amounts of any house plant fertilizer applied at four-month intervals will suffice to keep *Cissus* foliage healthy without encouraging too rapid growth. A soil composed of equal parts of loam, peat moss, and sand will meet their needs. *Cissus* do best when given abundant but filtered light.

Cissus antarctica (Vitis antarctica), Kangaroo Ivy, Kangaroo Vine

There is little doubt but that the Kangaroo Ivy should be close to the top of any list of tough indoor vines. Its glossy leaves, shaped like and much the size of those of Elm trees, are saw-toothed along the edges. Under house culture the Kangaroo Ivy does not grow too rapidly and will stay beautiful for a long while because even its older leaves continue to stay green and attractive. It is very well adapted to wall planters because the slow-growing stems descend in flowing lines, but the new growth at the tips always rises in a lithesome manner. In addition to the original species, there is a very appealing Miniature Kangaroo Ivy, *C. antarctica minima*, which has a very compact habit of growth with little tendency to climb.

The soil beneath Kangaroo Ivies should be kept moist, but not saturated.

Cissus discolor, Begonia Treebine

It may be that you have never seen the plant *Cissus discolor*, although specimens have been grown in conservatories for generations. Unlike other members of the family discussed in this section, this species requires a humid atmosphere in order to thrive, but its foliage is so remarkable that flower lovers continue to grow it in their homes with varying degrees of success. It is a rather fast-growing climber under congenial conditions of warmth and moisture and has spearhead-shaped leaves in a bewildering combination of colors. The base color might be described as a soft green, but each leaf is overlaid with violet, purple, and silvery zones and is etched by deep red veins. In addition, the backs of the leaves, the stems, and the leaf petioles are of a deep maroon shade. The common name, Begonia Treebine, is an allusion to the similarity of the foliage to that of Rex Begonias. *Cissus discolor* is native to the humid jungles of Java.

Cissus erosa

This Puerto Rican vine does not have an English name, since it is quite new to commercial horticulture. In habit it has much the appearance of Grape Ivy, since its waxy green foliage is three parted. It is a fast-growing climber which makes an excellent house plant. Keep the soil moist but not overly wet, for saturated conditions will cause this attractive plant to drop its foliage.

Cissus quadrangularis (*Vitis quadrangularis*), Winged Treebine

The specific name *quadrangularis* given to this succulent member of the Grape family alludes to the four-winged appearance of its stems. In arid parts of tropical Asia and Africa this plant often drops all of its grapelike leaves and then appears somewhat like a climbing member of the Cactus family. Give the Winged Treebine a bright sunny spot and dry loamy soil. It is often more unusual than ornamental, but it has a place in pot plant culture if only because there are relatively few plants which will grow under such dry and sunny conditions.

Cissus rhombifolia, Grape Ivy (See Plate 27.)

The fact that Grape Ivies have continued to delight generations of indoor gardeners proves that this species adapts superbly to house culture. Their shiny three-parted leaves are light to dark green above, with an attractive bronzy tint on new growth.

The reverse sides of the leaves, as well as the young stems, are surfaced with a fuzz of tiny soft brown hairs. Give Grape Ivies filtered light and keep the soil moist, but not wet. The leaves will be especially beautiful if you wash them occasionally with the sprayer at your kitchen sink. Grape Ivies are native to northern South America.

Cissus striata (*Vitis sempervirens*), Miniature Grape Ivy

This Chilean species has five-parted, palmately compound leaves which are bronzy green above and deep red below, especially on new shoots. This plant is truly a fine house species because of its small size and daintiness. The leaves, for example, though one and one half inches across, are made up of five tiny segments, and they add to the delicate lacy appearance of the plants. Keep the soil uniformly moist, but never soaking wet.

Ficus pumila and *Ficus radicans variegata*, see Chapter 2.

Hedera canariensis variegata, Variegated Canary Island Ivy (See Plate 28.)

Indoor gardeners in cold climates and outdoor gardeners in such mild areas as Southern California have found that few climbing plants are as attractive as the easy-to-grow Variegated Canary Island Ivy. This lovely species, sometimes sold under the name "Gloire de Marengo," will tolerate more warmth than will English Ivy, but in all other particulars its culture is similar.

Hedera helix (many varieties), English Ivy

It is astonishing to visit the greenhouse of a florist who makes a specialty of the newer forms of English Ivy. There are literally scores of superb types with all sorts of intriguing foliage from which to choose. Most varieties have dark green leaves, but certain ones are variegated with zones of white, yellow, or gray, and some even have tints of pink among the older leaves. No matter what their foliage differences, English Ivies are good house plants which may be trained to a support or allowed to drift over the side of a flowerpot in an airy way.

It should be said that English Ivies, in whatever varieties you grow them, will do best when given a rather cool site which is as humid as possible. It might be said that the damp cool weather of England, which is so much to their liking, ought to be your goal in choosing a place for them in your home. Most of us cannot provide such ideal conditions, but we can help the plants to health by spraying the foliage with water as often as possible. This is good for them, not only because it provides cool moisture on the leaves, but also because it washes away dust and insects from the foliage. In fact, regular forceful spraying with cold water is a good preventive method for keeping infestations of red spider mites to a minimum. These are about the only common insects which infest English Ivy. They congregate on the lower sides of the leaves and suck out cell juices, causing the leaves to turn yellow, especially when the plants are grown in warm locations. Plain cold water under pressure will wash them down the drain!

Give your English Ivies a soil composed of equal parts of loam, peat moss, and sand, and keep it pleasantly moist at all times. Feed them with any house plant fertilizer about three times a year. They will grow in full sun or quite deep shade, but they do best of all in bright light without direct sunshine.

Hoya carnosa, Wax Plant

For a great many years Wax Plants have been beloved house plants, and it is not uncommon to find large specimens either trained on a trellis or around an indoor window frame. Their name is an allusion to their lovely waxlike, fragrant pink blossoms. It is vital to realize that flower spurs should not be removed after blossoms fade because subsequent blossoms will appear from the same spurs.

Wax Plants of several species are native throughout the East Indies from northern Australia to southern China. This particular species, *H. carnosa,* has thick gray-green leaves, two to four inches long, which come to a point at each end. There are variegated-leafed mutations, one of the best being Exotica, whose leaves are widely marked with zones of white and occasional tinges of pink.

Wax Plants may grow to be six to eight feet tall, but are usually twined about a small trellis so as to make more compact specimens. They should have a sunny place, or one with abundant light. The soil should be given a thorough soaking, then allowed to become quite dry before the plants are watered again. It may be that some old plants which seem to do so well achieve their good health from the fact that their owners are neglectful and forget to water them too often!

Give Wax Plants a humusy soil composed of equal parts of rich loam, peat moss, leaf mold, and sharp sand.

Piper, Pepper Vine

Pepper vines, most of which come from the East Indies, are beginning to find their rightful place on the limited list of ornamental climbers suited for house culture. The most familiar member of this family is *Piper nigrum,* an Indonesian vine from which both black and white peppers are derived. Black pepper is made from the dried pulpy outer parts of the seeds, and white pepper comes from the inner white sections. Pepper is believed to have been the first spice used by mankind. *P. nigrum* has shiny, elliptical leaves which are black-green in color. It does well in the home, but its leaves are not as colorful as those of the following species: *P. ornatum* has deep green heart-shaped leaves, richly laced with silvery pink. *P. porphyrophyllum* received its name because its moss-green leaves are studded with sharply etched pink zones reminiscent of the way in which porphyry is marked. The undersides of the leaves, as well as the stems, are deep red in color. *P. crocatum,* from

Peru, has rather slender, shiny, quilted leaves whose veins are chased with silvery pink, and whose reverse sides are purple.

Pepper vines need a moist humusy soil and shelter from the direct sun. A mixture made of two parts peat moss and one part each of loam and sand will meet their needs. They are not rampant climbers as house plants, but will ascend a light trellis or may be allowed to trail gracefully from a hanging basket or wall bracket.

Senecio mikanioides, German or Parlor Ivy

German Ivy could easily be mistaken for English Ivy by a casual observer because the leaves are of very much the same shape. They are of a soft and succulent texture, however, and are of a much brighter green than English Ivy leaves. Mature plants send forth clusters of small bright yellow flowers.

Give German Ivies filtered light and a moist soil in a relatively cool location. The plants grow quite fast and can become too large for the house if they are not pruned to induce bushiness. Plants which are tip-pruned regularly develop into attractive compact specimens which make fine house plants. Give them a not too rich soil made up of loam, peat moss, and sand. German Ivies are from South Africa and are closely related to Cinerarias.

Vinca, Periwinkle

The most commonly grown trailing plant for summer window boxes is the Mottled Bigleaf Periwinkle, *V. major variegata.* Although it is not winter hardy in cold areas and does well in sunny or partly shaded indoor locations, it is seldom grown as a house plant. It has much to recommend it, for, besides graceful trailing stems, which are ideal for hanging baskets, and attractively mottled green and white leaves, it has lovely azure flowers from spring until fall. An ordinary potting soil of peat moss, sand, and loam will please these accommodating plants pro-

PLATE 17

Chamaedorea elegans bella (Neanthe bella), Parlor Palm

Nephthytis Green Gold (*Syngonium podophyllum xanthophilum*), Green Gold Nephthytis

PLATE 18

PLATE 19

Podocarpus macrophylla maki, Maki Podocarpus

Pittosporum tobira variegata, Variegated Japanese Pittosporum

PLATE 20

PLATE 21

Spathiphyllum clevelandii, Cleveland Spathiphyllum

Nephrolepis exaltata, Fluffy Ruffles, Fluffy Ruffles Boston Fern

PLATE 22

PLATE 23

Monstera deliciosa (Philodendron pertusum), Swiss Cheese Plant

Aglaonema pseudo-bracteatum, Variegated Chinese Evergreen

PLATE 24

PLATE 25

Heartleaf Philodendron Climbing Massange Dracaena Totem Pole

Citrus mitis, Calamondin Orange

PLATE 26

PLATE 27

Cissus rhombifolia, Grape Ivy

Hedera canariensis variegata, Variegated Canary Island Ivy

PLATE 28

PLATE 29

Caladium hortulanum, Fancy-Leafed Caladium

Araucaria excelsa, Norfolk Island Pine

PLATE 30

PLATE 31

Pandanus veitchii, Veitch's Variegated Screw-Pine

Dish Garden

PLATE 32

vided they are kept barely moist at all times. In order to keep new growth coming, it is a good idea to feed them lightly about once a month during the spring and summer. Periwinkles come to us from the southern part of Europe.

Vitis antarctica, see *Cissus antarctica*

Vitis quadrangularis, see *Cissus quadrangularis*

Vitis sempervirens, see *Cissus striata*

CHAPTER 22

BIZARRE BROMELIADS

The idea of using Bromeliads as house plants is such a new one that most gardeners are vague as to what they really are. Perhaps it would be useful to point out that all of us are familiar with at least one Bromeliad, the Pineapple. Perhaps you have even rooted and grown the tuft of foliage from the top of a Pineapple and found it a satisfactory house plant. As a matter of fact, the rosette habit of growth in which Pineapples grow is typical of most members of the family. There is always, among the types grown as house plants, a central cup surrounded by rather stiff leaves. These leaves may lie flat upon the ground, as they do in many species of the genus *Cryptanthus*. In this case it has given rise to a common name of "Ground Star." Other genera are apt to be somewhat taller, with more arching leaves, but each has a central "vase" which not only is watertight, but should be kept filled with water at all times.

The idea of keeping standing water in the central cups of Bromeliads is one of the most difficult for many persons to accept. It seems against all nature, and it surely is against all we have learned about most house plants, but we have to realize that Bromeliads are different from other plants. While their culture is not what one would ordinarily expect, it is not at all complicated, and it should be known that Bromeliads are fine house plants.

In the first place, though some Bromeliads are terrestrial and grow on the jungle floor, most of them are epiphytes and grow on trees and rocks, to which they cling more for support than for nourishment. It is indicative of their tolerance, as well as the success that Bromeliad fanciers achieve, that recommended soil mixtures range all the way from well-decayed pine needles to peat moss, sphagnum moss, chunks of charcoal, ground fir bark, leaf mold, and Osmunda Fern fiber. In fact, some Bromeliads are complete epiphytes and need no soil at all. One may simply tie a plant to a bark-covered slab, keep the central cup filled with water, and it will prosper. Such species are not recommended for house culture, however, because they need higher humidity than most homes provide, but they do grow easily in a warm greenhouse.

It can be said that nearly all Bromeliads offered for sale as house plants prefer filtered light. Some will stand more exposure than others and under such conditions will exhibit brighter foliage colors. Never move a plant abruptly from deep shade into full sun, but experiment with your Bromeliads to see how much color their leaves take on as optimum light conditions are approached.

All Bromeliads are native to warm regions of the Americas, stretching from Florida deep into South America. They do best under the warm temperatures of our homes, but they will survive at readings as low as forty degrees Fahrenheit.

Bromeliad roots do little to supply food for the plants. It is believed that their chief function is to anchor the plants to the rough bark of jungle trees. In house plant culture this fact is recognized by potting them in what appear to be ridiculously small pots which supply just enough weight to keep the plants from toppling over on their sides.

In their native habitat Bromeliads often have frogs and other creatures living in the watery cups of the plants. Such is the strange relationship between plants and animals that it is believed that the minute droppings of these creatures supply most of the nourishment used by the plants. In commercial culture this idea has been capitalized upon by feeding the plants through their leaves. You may do the same in your home by filling the cups of your Bromeliads once a month with an extremely mild solution of a house plant fertilizer dissolved in water. Use no more than one-half strength of the weakest proportions stated on the directions for use of your favorite house plant fertilizer. Use rain water if possible; *never use softened water*. Wash Bromeliad cups occasionally with clear water so that excessive deposits of fertilizer salts will not accumulate.

In this book Bromeliads are discussed as foliage plants, not only because of their attractive leaves, but also because the greater part of their ornamental lives occurs before they blossom. They do have exotic flowers, but after they fade from a given rosette, the rosette dies away, and the foliage cycle begins again. Prior to its death, however, each rosette gives rise to a number of basal offshoots which may be removed and grown on to maturity. It is in this stage of their life before flowering that we are most interested here, for Bromeliad foliage is some of the most exceptional in the world. Basic leaf colors may be any shade of green, gray, or almost brown, but it is often striped, barred, zebra-marked, or spotted with other colors. These colors, as mentioned previously, are greatly accentuated by additional light. Even more important, many Bromeliads take on brilliant hues, especially reds, toward the centers of the plants as they mature.

The following Bromeliads, which are the ones most often found in flower shops, are the types most suited to house plant culture.

Aechmea, Aechmea

Among all the Bromeliads grown in homes, Aechmeas are the most common. Their leaves may be green or greenish red, or green-and-white combinations. Flowers are usually red and yellow, often with touches of blue. They like light shade.

Ananas, Pineapple

Miniature Pineapple plants are often sold by florists, complete with tiny fruit growing on the central stems which rise from each rosette of long leaves. Pineapples do best if given full sun.

Billbergia, Billbergia

Most Billbergias are ridiculously easy to grow and have queer pendant clusters of red, green, and blue flowers on mature plants. They can stand full sun or bright reflected light.

Cryptanthus, Cryptanthus, "Ground Star"

If you have a dish garden, there is a very good chance that it contains a Cryptanthus, for these little ground-hugging fellows are ideal as the lowest growing specimens in such a combination. Their foliage is green, beige, or tan and is usually marked with zebralike stripes across the leaves. They like filtered light.

Dyckia, Dyckia

Most of the Dyckias in cultivation have orange or yellow flowers and narrow spiny-edged leaves which recurve in a nearly circular manner. They like protection from the sun.

Neoregelia, Neoregelia, Fingernail Plant

One of the favorite Neoregelias is called Fingernail Plant because the tips of its leaves appear to have been touched with a bright red fingernail polish. Many other Neoregelias have brightly colored center leaves on mature plants. All like partly shaded locations.

Nidularium, Nidularium

The flowers of this genus are borne deep down among the leaves, which someone has likened to a nest. This accounts for its botanical name which comes from the Latin *nidus,* meaning nest. This type of Bromeliad should be given light shade.

Tillandsia, Tillandsia

The epiphyte Spanish Moss, which you have seen growing on trees and even telephone wires in the South, is a Tillandsia, but most other members of the family spring from rosettes. Gray green is the predominant foliage color, but lavender flowers spring from paddle-shaped flower heads composed of pink, yellow, or red bracts. Protect Tillandsias from the full sun.

Vriesia, Vriesia

This genus produces some of the most startling of house plants. The foliage may be nearly any shade of green and is usually spotted, barred, or marbled with other colors. Paddle-shaped flower spikes may be purple, red, or yellow. One favorite Vriesia is called Flaming Sword. Give them filtered light.

CHAPTER 23

MINOR FOLIAGE PLANTS

The term *minor foliage plants* may not seem to be a fair one because your favorite plant may be on the list, yet some spot must be found to group together a host of plants which are of lesser importance in the over-all picture of indoor foliage plants. Some of the plants included here are excellent commonly grown house plants; some are fine species which deserve more publicity; others are exotically beautiful things, but they are at their best in a warm, humid greenhouse and must be given special attention if they are to survive in the home. These unusual conditions are set forth in Chapter 26, Terrariums and Indoor Greenhouses.

You will find it difficult to locate some of these plants, either because they are new to commerce or because florists have not had sufficient call for them to make it profitable to stock them. One thing is certain: Until more flower lovers know about them and ask for them, they will not be generally available.

A considerable number of the minor plants have attractive or unique flowers which are often borne in house culture. This cannot be said for the greater number of larger foliage plants, which rely entirely upon their foliage for their charm. In addition, it must be stressed that everyone does not have sufficient space for large-growing foliage plants. Here he may find fascinating miniatures to fit his growing space as well as to satisfy his longing for living plants.

Acanthus, Acanthus, Bears-Breech, Mountain Thistle

Ancient Greeks were so fascinated with the shape of Acanthus leaves that they used them as models in the design of the capitals of Corinthian columns. Architects and sculptors today continue to use the Acanthus motif in their work. Several species are native to the region bordering on the Mediterranean. *A. mollis* is a two-foot perennial herb with large, glossy, nonspiny, deeply lobed leaves topped with small spikes of lilac-colored flowers. *A. montanus,* sometimes known as Mountain Thistle, becomes a three-foot shrub and has spiny, pinnatifid* leaves so dark green as to seem almost black. Its flowers are rose tinted. Acanthuses do well as tub plants because of the spreading nature of their large leaves. They should be given filtered light and a barely moist loamy soil mixture of which one third should be organic material such as very well-decayed manure or peat moss. Since they do not become taller as they increase in age, regular feedings with a house plant fertilizer every three or four months are in order. Plants which finally exhaust the soil in their containers can be repotted in fresh soil.

Anthurium, Tailflower, Flamingo Flower

The glistening heart-shaped red, pink, or white flowers of Anthuriums, punctuated by their erect or twisted "tails," are among the most exotic sold by florists, and it is natural that home gardeners would like to have them as house plants. In Europe they are very popular for this purpose, but here most of our homes lack the high humidity necessary for their culture. They can be grown very successfully in indoor greenhouses or terrariums where high humidity can be maintained, but, except in humid sections, they are not satisfactory as ordinary house plants.

* Cleft in a pinnate manner, with narrow lobes not reaching to the midrib.

There are hundreds of species of Anthuriums native to the jungles of northern South America. Of these, two are suitable for house culture when proper conditions can be provided. *A. andraeanum* and its varieties have erect "tails" and red, pink, or white flowers. *A. scherzerianum* is often called Flamingo Flower because of its twisted spadices. This species is generally smaller growing than the preceding one and is to be recommended for terrarium culture. All Anthurium blossoms last for weeks and are truly exceptional flowers.

Several Anthuriums are grown in greenhouses for their amazing foliage. Of these the most popular is *A. crystallinum*, whose large velvety-green, white-veined leaves seem to have crystals imbedded in their upper surfaces.

Anthuriums should be potted in a mixture of Osmunda fiber, sand, and old cow manure, or sphagnum moss, leaf mold, and pieces of charcoal. It should be kept constantly moist, but not saturated. Plants blossom only when growing; so they should be fed lightly once a month with a complete house plant fertilizer.

It is necessary that Anthuriums be kept warm and out of the sun, as well as under highly humid conditions.

Aphelandra, Aphelandra

Central and South American jungles are home to several species of Aphelandras, but only one of them is commonly offered by florists. This is the one known as *Aphelandra squarrosa louisae*, whose shiny green leaves, etched by clear white veins, would make it an outstanding plant even if it were not favored with huge terminal clusters of bright yellow flowers in the autumn. Two other species without showy foliage but with bright flowers are *A. aurantiaca*, whose blossoms are orange, and *A. tetragona*, which has bright scarlet blooms. All Aphelandras like a moist, humusy soil made of two parts peat moss and one part each of loam and sand. Generally speaking, new plants should be started from cuttings in the spring and grown through the year for a brilliant autumn display. Plants should be kept warm and shielded from direct sun.

Aralia, see *Dizygotheca, Fatsia, Polyscias, Tetrapanax* (formerly known as *Aralia* species)

Asparagus sprengeri, Sprengeri-Fern

The Sprengeri-Fern, unlike its climbing relative, the Asparagus-Fern, discussed in Chapter 21, does not climb, but has gracefully arching, ferny, though thorny, branches up to two feet long. Its foliage is rich green and needlelike, thus is particularly beautiful in a hanging basket where the stems can cascade on all sides. It has small fragrant white flowers followed by bright red berries.

The Sprengeri-Fern grows from tuberous roots, which may be easily divided to procure more plants, or plants may be grown from seeds. They do best with light protection from the sun and should be given a moist soil composed of equal parts peat moss, loam, and sand.

Aspidistra elatior (A. lurida), Cast Iron Plant

As the name would imply, the Cast Iron Plant is one that will take all sorts of abuse. It is a member of the Lily family and has long, slender dark green leaves, except for the variety *variegata,* whose leaves are striped with green and white. Plants grow about eighteen inches tall and are not particular as to soil conditions, but do best in a moist mixture of equal parts of peat moss, loam, and sand. Aspidistras are plants for "impossible" situations, for they will tolerate dark corners, drafts, and low temperatures as long as they are above freezing.

Beaucarnea recurvata (Nolina tuberculata), Beaucarnea

We are indebted to arid regions of Mexico and Texas for this exotic member of the Lily family we call Beaucarnea. In many ways it is somewhat similar to such plants as Yucca and

Spanish Dagger because it has terminal clusters of long, narrow, tough leaves and panicles of small whitish flowers. This plant has the specific name of *B. recurvata* to denote that its leaves are so long that they recurve in the manner of ram's horns. Its most peculiar trait is the bulbous nature of the base of its treelike stem. In the desert Beaucarneas may go for a year without rain. For this reason it is wise to keep the soil beneath them quite dry most of the time. They can stand wide extremes of temperature and should have bright light or full sun to do their best. A loamy soil will suit their needs. An annual light feeding of a house plant fertilizer applied in early spring will meet their nutritional requirements. Young plants may be grown in ordinary flowerpots, but older specimens become large enough to require tub culture.

Begonia (several varieties), Begonia

The Begonia family is an immense one, and although all of its members have flowers, certain types are grown primarily for their attractive foliage. These are the groups under consideration here. They include such colorful forms as the Rex Begonia and other rhizomatous types, the Cane-stemmed or Angel Wing Begonias, which have spectacular flower clusters as well as attractive leaves, the Hairy-Leafed Begonias, and several unclassified species and hybrids.

The Rex Begonias, despite their wondrous beauty, are plants which are not particularly easy to grow. What they really like is the humid warmth of a tropical greenhouse in order to do their best. In the home one should strive to give them conditions as close to these as possible, which include considerable protection from strong light, as well as a soil that is constantly barely moist.

The rest of the group in question are more amenable to house culture. They can grow very well under less humidity, and they like the soil to become nearly dry between waterings. In addition, they like a good deal of light such as they would receive in a spot just out of the direct sun.

Begonias enjoy a humusy but well-drained soil. One composed of loam, peat moss, leaf mold, and sand in equal parts will do very well. They do not need a great deal of fertilizer. A light dusting of bone meal can be added to the potting mixture, and mild feedings of a house plant fertilizer can be applied every two to three months.

Buxus, Boxwood

It may come as a surprise to you to find Boxwood listed as a foliage plant for the home, but the Dwarf English Boxwood, *Buxus sempervirens suffruticosa,* is commonly used in dish gardens and terrariums. Its small leaves and slow habit of growth, its ability to live in dark places, as well as light ones, and in cold areas, as well as warm ones, commends this little plant to indoor culture. Any ordinary potting soil will meet its needs.

Caladium hortulanum, Caladium, Fancy-Leafed Caladium (See Plate 29.)

It is only fair to consider Caladiums as part-time foliage plants, for, though they are spectacular plants during their growing season, they die down to the ground for a dormant period of several months each year.

Once you have seen a Caladium, you will never fail to recognize another one. It is true that many plants have leaves shaped like those of Caladiums, but the moment color enters the picture, other factors become irrelevant. Caladium leaves look like huge broad-based arrowheads; they are papery in texture and often have prominent veining. Leaf color, the most distinguishing characteristic of Caladiums, is difficult to describe because of the extreme variability among plants and even among leaves on the same plant. In general it might be said that leaf colors range through shades of pink, white, green, and red;

thus it is easy to understand how they came to be called Fancy-Leafed Caladiums.

Caladiums come from the tropical jungles of Colombia, where the climate is divided into wet and dry seasons. This gives us a clue to their life cycles, for while they appear to be permanent foliage plants, they actually have only a seasonal period of above-ground growth. In greenhouses dormant roots may be started into growth at any time of year. Thus we see them at midwinter flower shows as well as in flower shops in midsummer, but a given plant cannot perform at both seasons. Summer Caladiums are started into growth in early spring and are at their loveliest during midsummer. By late fall they cease making new leaves and gradually lose the older ones.

Caladiums enjoy a moist soil composed of equal parts of peat moss and sandy loam. They like to be warm at all times (65 to 80° Fahrenheit) and will grow in full sun or partial shade. Feed them every two weeks with a very dilute house plant fertilizer so that the leaves will be large and colorful and the plants will store up energy in their roots for another season. As they approach their rest period, water should be withheld and the roots should be stored in a warm, dry place until the following spring.

Calathea, Calathea, Peacock Plant, Zebra Plant

Some of the most decorative foliage plants known to horticulture may be found in the Calathea family, but few homes can provide the humidity that Calatheas need to do their best. It is a plant with which to experiment to see if you can provide proper growing conditions. Calatheas are closely related to Prayer Plants, *Maranta,* and display the same gorgeously marked foliage, but to a greater extent and on larger plants. Many varieties have a basic leaf color shading toward chartreuse. They are generously marked, usually along lateral veins, with wide brush strokes of opaque olive green or near-brown. The undersides of the leaves are often a shade of deep wine red or purple. Give Calatheas a moist humusy soil made of two parts peat moss and one part each of loam and sand. They like a warm location which is protected from the direct sun. Most Calatheas come from the humid jungles of northern South America and as house plants grow one to three feet tall.

Callisia elegans (Setcreasea striata), Callisia

Horticultural literature of even a few years ago does not list this attractive little creeping plant from Mexico, whose habit of growth shows that it is a Wandering Jew relative. Its leaves are green above but brightly striped with closely set white lines which run the length of each leaf. The undersurfaces are reddish purple in color. This species should be given a spot out of the sun and a humusy soil which is kept evenly moist at all times.

Ceropegia woodii, String of Hearts, Rosary Vine

Botanists have found many species of *Ceropegia* growing in parts of Africa and the Canary Islands, but only one is generally found in flower shops. This is the trailing vine *Ceropegia woodii*, a charming species with stringlike stems and tiny, thick, heart-shaped, mottled gray-green-pink leaves. Among the leaves one may occasionally find their waxy pinkish-purple flowers. Grow these plants in partial shade and let them dry out somewhat between waterings. They do well in a soil composed of equal parts of loam, peat moss, and sand. They do not grow rapidly and take but little space. Give them a shelf location so that their stems may hang down where they can be seen and appreciated.

Chamaeranthemum, Chamaeranthemum

Growers of terrariums or indoor greenhouses will welcome three South American species of Chamaeranthemums, small-foliaged creeping plants whose leaves are variously marked with odd colorations. They thrive only under the highly humid conditions of a tropical greenhouse or terrarium, thus are not usually satisfactory house plants when grown in average household situations. *C. gaudichaudii* has broad silvery sections in each leaf, marking midrib and major veins; *C. igneum* has velvety, brownish-green leaves with red-to-yellow veins, and *C. venosum* has a delicate tracery of silver etching the veining of its leaves. An average house plant soil will suit Chamaeranthemums provided it is kept moist at all times. Their flowers, lavender or yellow, according to the species, are borne in small terminal racemes. Give them light shade.

Chlorophytum, Spider Plant, Ribbon Plant, Bracket Plant

This grassy-tufted house plant has been grown for generations and is of such easy culture and propagation and is so widespread among flower lovers that few florists bother to stock it. It has long blades of foliage much like that of Daylilies, except that they are striped with areas of white or yellow. Several species and varieties are to be found, all of which produce plantlets on the ends of flower stalks. When the tiny white flowers fade, the young plants continue to grow, becoming heavy enough to bend the stalks over to the ground where the small plants quickly root. When grown on a wall bracket or as a hanging-basket plant, the young plants are not able to touch soil, so are gracefully pendant on arching stems about the mother plant.

In addition to this normal way of producing new plants, the tuberous roots may be divided. Repot them in a mixture of equal parts of loam, peat moss, and sand. Keep the soil moist at all times and grow the plants in filtered light.

Coffea, Coffee

Although Coffee bushes are not often grown as ornamental plants, they surely are interesting if only as conversation pieces.

All species have attractive, but thin and easily marred, glossy, dark green leaves. Bushes often develop several stems and in the tropics become as much as fifteen feet tall, but in the home they may be kept at any height desired by pinching out terminal shoots as they develop. Coffee blossoms are tiny, white, and exceedingly fragrant and are followed by red or black berries. These contain twin seeds, which, when cured, roasted, and ground, are the basis for the beverage we enjoy. Coffee bushes do well in an organically rich loamy soil which should be kept barely moist at all times. Give them bright light, but not full sun.

Coleus, Coleus

It may be that you think of Coleus plants as being summer bedding subjects, but it is true that they are likewise very easy-to-grow plants for sunny or lightly shaded indoor locations. The variation in leaf colors staggers the imagination, and one may choose nearly any color or combination of colors to suit his taste.

Two types of Coleuses are grown: The most common one is the upright form descended from *Coleus blumei,* a native of Java; the delightful trailing kinds are selections of *Coleus rehneltianus* from Ceylon. It is this latter type which is responsible for the long-popular variety Trailing Queen, as well as others of the same growth characteristics.

Coleuses like warm temperatures and a moist, humusy soil. When plants become too large, it is an easy matter to start young ones from cuttings.

Costus, Spiral Ginger, Spiral Flag, Stepladder Plant

Four members of the Spiral Ginger family have lately come into limited use as foliage plants. Their chief appeal lies in the odd way in which their attractive leaves are arranged spirally around their slender stems. They do well in warm locations under light shade. Give them a moist loamy soil mixture of which one third is peat moss. Spiral Gingers are ornamental even as young plants, but become striking as large tub-grown specimens. Root-bound clumps may be divided and repotted into fresh soil. *C. igneus* has maroon stems, leaves which are green above, but reddish beneath, and bright orange flowers. This Brazilian perennial becomes three feet tall. *C. malortieanus* (*C. zebrinus*) from Costa Rica also grows to a height of three feet. Its large hairy green leaves are marked by lengthwise stripes of darker hue. This species has yellow flowers marked with red. The leaves of *C. sanguineus,* another Central American species, have prominent silvery midribs and are deep red beneath. An Indian member of the family *C. speciosus* becomes ten feet tall in its native land, but as a house plant it usually is seen as a two- to three-foot specimen.

Crassula, Jade Plant

One of the most commonly grown house plants is the succulent *Crassula argentea,* or Jade Plant, sold commercially under the name of *C. arborescens* because even small plants take on the shape of little trees. In addition to the species, which has thick silvery-green leaves, there are several varieties, among which the most notable are *variegata,* with leaves mottled green and creamy white, and *tricolor,* whose foliage is similar to the above except that the leaves are margined in red. Jade Plants are native to the dry regions of South Africa and do well in either bright sun or light shade. A dry loamy soil suits their needs as growing plants, but strangely enough, they will also live for long periods of time in plain water. Occasionally Jade Plants will blossom in the house, rewarding the gardener with clusters of tiny white flowers which turn pinkish as they age. Indoor specimens usually average under twelve inches in height, but old plants may become three or four feet tall.

Dichorisandra mosaica undata, see *Geogenanthus undatus*

Dichorisandra reginae, Dichorisandra

If you should find a plant at your florist's shop which looks something like a Wandering Jew, but has silvery-banded leaves which are purple on the reverse side, you probably will have found a *Dichorisandra reginae.* It has no common name, but it is a colorful, relatively new addition to the small-plant field and does best in a warm, partly shaded location in moist, humusy soil.

Dizygotheca (Aralia), False Aralia

The False Aralia has dark reddish-copper palmately compound leaves which are quite reminiscent of the foliage of cut-leaf forms of the red Japanese Maple. Its airy grace and upright growth habit assure it a lasting place as an interesting foliage plant. Two types are to be found: *D. elegantissima* from the New Hebrides and *D. veitchii* from New Caledonia. Both make fine house plants. Give them a soil mixture of two parts peat moss and one part each of loam and sand. Keep the soil moist at all times and protect the plants from direct sun.

Episcia, Flame Violet, Episcia

Someone tried to climb on the African-Violet bandwagon by promoting red-flowered forms of the distantly related species *Episcia* as Flame Violet. In reality, Episcias are fully able to stand on their own merits as delightful house plants. There are an amazing number of species and hybrids, most of which grow somewhat in the manner of Strawberry plants, sending out runners on which plantlets appear at intervals. This feature makes Episcias natural choices for situations where the trailing stems can be most effectively displayed. There are many leaf colors available, often with quilted texture, ranging from bronze to green, some of which are marked with silver or pink. Their small blossoms may be red, yellow, pink, lilac, or white. Give the plants partial shade, an evenly moist soil made up of equal parts of peat moss, leaf mold, rich loam, and sharp sand. A mild house plant fertilizer should be given every three to four weeks except from November until mid-February, when the plants make little growth. If you find that the air in your house is too dry for Episcias, grow them in a terrarium. You will find that they are real gems.

Euonymous, Euonymous

Most of us think of Euonymous as garden shrubs or vines, but young plants of *E. japonicus* are excellent indoor subjects, most frequently used in dish gardens in conjunction with other plants. There are, in addition to the green-leafed forms, others with markings of yellow or white. They prefer a cool site, an evenly moist soil mixture made of equal parts of peat moss, sand, and loam, and protection from the full sun. Euonymous foliage benefits from syringing with a forceful spray to remove dust and discourage attacks by red spider mites.

Fatsia japonica (*Aralia sieboldii*), Fatsia

Fatsias are surely not minor plants as far as size is concerned, for they are really bold evergreen shrubs from Japan with immense palmately lobed, leathery leaves. In effect, Fatsias give much the same impression as do Scheffleras, to which they are related. They prefer cool conditions and can tolerate temperatures as low as forty degrees Fahrenheit, but they do not make active growth except at higher temperatures. Give them bright light, but not full sun, and keep the soil beneath them moist at all times. Fatsias like a rich, loamy soil well supplied with peat moss or leaf mold. Feed them lightly every three to four months to maintain healthy leaves without forcing luxuriant growth. A more compact Fatsia is the variety *moseri;* a type with green and creamy-white foliage is known as *variegata.*

Fittonia, Fittonia

These attractive plants are included in this section only because they do well in terrariums or indoor greenhouses, not because they are satisfactory as ordinary house plants. Two species are commonly grown: *F. verschaffeltii* has deep green leaves and red veining, while *F. verschaffeltii argyoneura* has bright green leaves with silvery veins. Both need a highly humid situation and quite heavy shading. Plants creep along the ground, never becoming more than a few inches tall. Give them a moist humusy soil made of half peat moss or leaf mold, plus one-fourth part each of sand and loam.

Geogenanthus undatus (Dichorisandra mosaica undata), Seersucker Plant

Once you have met this appealing little Peruvian plant with its homespun name, you will agree that it has a bright future ahead as a house plant. The name Seersucker Plant is an extremely appropriate one, since the surface of each leaf is puckered and ridged in much the same manner as the cloth which bears the same name. Upper leaf surfaces have silvery veins running lengthwise over a blackish-green background, and the undersides of the leaves, as well as the stems, are wine red in color.

Seersucker Plants branch freely from the base, soon making bushy little specimens six to ten inches tall and fully as broad. They should be given protection from direct sunshine and a soil that is moist and high in humus. Many commercial growers produce their plants in pure peat moss or a mixture of half peat moss and one fourth each of loam and sand. Situations that suit African Violets will please Seersucker Plants as well. They are members of the *Tradescantia* or Spiderwort family and occasionally have small violet-colored flowers deeply set among the foliage.

Grevillea robusta, Silk-Oak

Silk-Oaks become one hundred fifty feet tall in their native Australia, but we grow them as house plants for their delicate fernlike foliage, which clings well to even the older growth. They like a bright, sunny location and should be allowed to dry a bit between waterings. A soil mixture of equal parts of loam, sand, and peat moss will fill their needs. It should be mentioned that they will outgrow a home after a season or two and should be discarded in favor of fresh young seedlings.

Gynura aurantiaca, Velvet Plant

Indoor gardeners are easily attracted to this showy plant, whose thick leaves are covered by a dense mat of bright purple hairs. It is a sun lover and should be given a bright spot and an evenly moist soil. A standard soil mixture of one third each of loam, sand, and peat moss will serve well. Under such conditions Velvet Plants will grow rapidly, and perhaps this is the chief factor against them, for it is hard for many flower lovers to bear to pinch out the lush growth to induce bushiness. Unless this is done, however, they tend to grow quite tall and leggy. Well-grown plants eventually send out orange flowers which clearly show their kinship to Daisies.

Heimerliodendron brunonianum variegatum (Pisonia grandis tricolor), Variegated Bird Catcher Tree

At first glance one might think that the Variegated Bird Catcher Tree is another member of the Rubber Tree family, for its leaves are of somewhat the same shape. However, this colorful plant, new to ornamental horticulture, is a mutation of an unrelated species native to the islands of the South Pacific from Tahiti to New Zealand and Australia. Its glossy leaves, under house culture, grow from six to ten inches long and two to three inches wide and, on a base of two-toned green, are strikingly marked with areas of cream, white, and pink. The ribs of the leaves, as well as the seed pods borne on mature trees, are sticky, giving rise to the name Bird Catcher Tree. Give this lovely plant light shade and an evenly moist soil composed of equal parts of loam, peat moss, and sand. Feed two to three times a year with a mild house plant fertilizer. Although Bird Catcher Trees may become large in time, they can easily be kept within bounds by pruning.

Hemigraphis, Hemigraphis

The moist and shady jungles of Java have yielded the noteworthy creeping herb we call *Hemigraphis colorata*. It has small reddish-purple scallop-edged leaves which have a gleaming metallic sheen. The plant is a robust grower when happy and roots into the soil as it increases in size. It often sends up little spikes of tiny white flowers. Hemigraphis is a plant to use in terrariums and indoor greenhouses, provided it is not allowed to encroach upon others. Pinch it back as often as necessary. It will also grow in clear water and is beautiful cascading from a hanging basket or wall bracket. It likes a constantly moist loamy soil and must never receive direct sunlight.

Hibiscus, Hibiscus

Most forms of Hibiscus are grown for their spectacular flowers, but one variety, *Hibiscus rosa-sinensis cooperi,* Cooper's Chinese Hibiscus, is unusual in that it is grown primarily for its attractively marked green and white leaves. The small scarlet flowers are a bonus. This plant should have a rich soil composed of equal parts of peat moss, loam, and sand and should be fed every two months to encourage fresh new growth.

It can easily be kept small by pinching off terminal shoots. Give Hibiscuses bright sunshine and a soil which is barely moist at all times.

Homalocladium (*Muehlenbeckia*), Ribbon Bush, Tapeworm Plant

This oddity from the Solomon Islands has been delighting gardeners for many years, although it is not widely grown. It is so preposterous as to be nearly unbelievable, for its stems are perfectly flat, one half inch wide, and leafless during the season that its little greenish flowers appear. During the balance of the year it puts out sparse willowy foliage. The plants may become two to four feet tall and should be given a moist, loamy soil and a bright sunny location.

Homalomena, Homalomena

Homalomenas are attractive foliage plants which share some of the characteristics of Caladiums and Dieffenbachias. Although various species are native to Indonesia as well as Colombia, only two South American types, plus a clone of one of them, ordinarily are grown. *H. picturata*, which might pass for a Caladium, has a broad band of silvery white down the center of each leaf. *H. wallisii*, with its silvery-yellow marked leaves, looks very much like a Dieffenbachia. A seedling of *H. wallisii* known as *mauro* is extensively marked with chartreuse marbling. Homalomenas like a moist soil of one half peat moss and one fourth each of loam and sand. Give them a warm location and semishade.

Hypoestes sanguinolenta, Freckleface, Pink Polka Dot

Either of the common names of this friendly little plant from Malagasy ought to ensure its acceptance among home gardeners. In its wild form the oval dark green leaves are unevenly spotted with pink dots, but two of the improved selections, Pink Brocade and Splash, are much more brightly colored, especially when grown in bright light. They do best when grown in a moist soil which is highly organic. A mixture of one half peat moss and one fourth each of sand and loam will suit their needs. It should be noted that these plants are apt to grow nearly three feet tall in an ungainly fashion unless tips of new shoots are pinched out to promote bushiness. They bear terminal clusters of tiny rosy-lavender flowers.

Kalanchoe, Kalanchoe, Air Plant, Panda Plant

It is easy to get bogged down in a discussion of a family of plants which is as large as Kalanchoe. For that reason we have chosen only three pot-sized species which are usually grown for their foliage rather than flowers. They are related to the red-flowered Kalanchoe, *K. blossfeldiana,* which is a popular house plant during the Christmas season. Kalanchoes should have a dry soil composed of equal parts of peat moss, sand, and loam and should be grown in bright sunny locations. *K. pinnata,* also known as *Bryophyllum,* has the common name of Air Plant because, when one of its broad succulent leaves is pinned to a curtain, it sends out a whole colony of miniature plants from the scalloped edges of the leaf, without ever receiving added moisture or touching the soil. A similar species is *K. tubiflora,* whose tiny purple-spotted leaves look like little cylinders. New plants form at the tips of its leaves. Such asexual propagation is known as viviparity, which means to bear living young. Perhaps the most interesting of the trio is the one commonly called Panda Plant, *K. tomentosa,* which means woolly. Its leaves are thickly covered with a whitish felt of tiny hairs, marked along the tips of their scalloped edges with dark brown hairs in the manner of a Panda. The Air Plant is native to India, and the others come from Malagasy, but all have spread to tropical lands around the world.

Maranta, Prayer Plant

Prayer Plants are among the smaller, nicer foliage plants suitable for situations where low stature is necessary. The broadly spreading, oddly marked foliage which hugs the sides of the pots is the typical growth habit during daylight hours. At night, however, plants raise their leaves heavenward as though in prayer, giving rise to the common name.

Two species of Maranta are commonly grown as house plants. *M. leuconeura kerchoveana* has a row of chocolate-colored blotches on either side of the midrib of each leaf, and *M. leuconeura massangeana* has a sharply etched silvery veinous marking against a darker background which reminds one of the skeleton of a fish. These strange plants come to us from the jungles of South America, and though they would enjoy more humidity than most households afford, they will still do well as indoor plants. They need shade in order to thrive.

A soil mixture composed of half peat moss, plus quarter parts each of loam and sand, kept moist from early spring until late in October, will suit their needs. During this time they benefit from a bimonthly feeding of a mild house plant fertilizer. During the balance of the year the soil should be barely moist, somewhat on the dry side. Plants may be divided in early spring. Occasionally they send out tiny flower spikes topped by inconspicuous white blossoms.

Pandanus, Screw-Pine

Any serviceman who made landings on South Pacific islands is acquainted with Screw-Pines, for these rugged relatives of Palms have long, pendant, spine-edged leaves and thick prop roots which jut out from the trunks of large plants. Certain species of Screw-Pines have long been used as indoor plants in public buildings or other areas where they have room to spread their leaves without interference from persons passing by. Even young plants cover an area three feet across, and mature specimens can be quite large.

All of the leaves of Screw-Pines arise spirally (thus the name Screw-Pine) from terminal growths and form large tufts of foliage, which is either entirely green or striped with yellow or white against a green background. The most popular species is *P. veitchii* (See Plate 31.), which has creamy-white lines on its leaves, and *P. veitchii compacta,* a more dwarf type with pure white markings. Another species often seen is *P. sanderi roehrsianus,* whose large leaves are attractively striped with yellow and green.

Screw-Pines do well in a soil mixture of one half peat moss and one quarter each of loam and sand. This mixture should be watered thoroughly, then be allowed to dry somewhat before more moisture is applied. Plants will do well in full sun or light shade. Feeding should be limited to two or three times a year so as not to force too rapid growth.

Pedilanthus, Devil's Backbone

This common pot plant gets its name from the zigzag manner in which the stems are formed. The most colorful species is *P. tithymaloides variegata* from the West Indies. Its waxy pale green leaves are brightly marked with white and touches of red. Small red flowers are occasionally borne at the tips of the stems. It can stand sunshine part of the day, but does best under filtered light and is more apt to hold its leaves under these conditions. Devil's Backbone does well in a barely moist soil made up of equal parts of sand, peat moss, and loam.

Pellionia, Pellionia

Pellionias are subjects for terrariums because they need the warmth and humidity of their Malaysian-jungle background in order to do well. The most common species found is *P. daveau-*

ana, a creeping plant with small oval bronzy-green leaves with broad veinous markings of olive green to gray. Give them warmth, shade, and a moist humusy soil.

Peperomia, Peperomia, Pepperface

If you are even a casual collector of indoor plants, you probably already have at least one Peperomia. What is more, there is a good chance that it has already lasted longer than any of your other house plants, particularly if you have been a bit neglectful about watering it! Plantsmen say that there are over five hundred different kinds of Peperomias which are native to parts of Central and South America. Nearly all are alike in at least two respects: Their leaves are apt to be orbicular in outline and somewhat fleshy; and most important of all, they desire similar growing conditions.

Peperomias like a bit of shade at all times and a soil that is allowed to dry out between waterings. Too much water, in fact, is about the only common reason for persons to lose their Peperomias. They like a soil which contains equal parts of loam, sand, and peat moss. It need not be overly fertile, since this would foster excessive growth. Mild feedings of a house plant fertilizer every three to four months are ample for their needs.

Three species of Peperomias account for a huge proportion of all the kinds grown in this country. The smallest of them is *Peperomia caperata.* Several selected forms exist, all with tiny, rich-looking foliage carefully pleated in accordion fashion. The next Peperomia in size is the ever-present *Peperomia obtusifolia* and its varieties. Its stems may get eight to twelve inches tall before bending gracefully from their weight of fleshy leaves, which may be clear green or marked attractively with yellow or white. The last commercially important species is *Peperomia sandersii,* known to many as Watermelon-Begonia because its leaves are marked with curving silvery bands in the manner of many Watermelons.

Phormium, New Zealand Flax

Any gardener expecting to find a resemblance between New Zealand Flax and the lovely blue-flowered Flax from which Irish linen is prepared is due for a surprise. New Zealand Flax looks like gigantic wide-bladed grass and forms, when grown in warm climates, stout clumps which may tower over a man's head. It is amenable to pot or tub culture, however, and is apt to be under three feet in height under these conditions. In addition to the brownish-green species, *P. tenax,* there are two interesting variations known as *atropurpureum,* which has reddish-purple leaves, and *variegatum,* whose foliage is marked with stripes of white and yellow. New Zealand Flax should have full sun and a moist soil composed of equal parts of loam, sand, and peat moss.

Pilea (several species, including Aluminum Plant, South American Friendship Plant, Artillery Plant, and others)

It is not easy to generalize about a plant family such as *Pilea,* whose members are so unlike one another, yet it can be said that many of them are attractive low-growing plants suitable for house culture, although some are happier in terrariums where high humidity can be maintained. All Pileas need filtered light and abundant moisture in a highly organic soil, preferably half peat moss, plus loam and sand.

Pilea cadierei, Aluminum Plant

This species and its dwarf variety, *minima,* are called Aluminum Plants because their quilted leaves appear to have been lightly brushed with aluminum paint on the raised portions. They grow rapidly and should be pinched often to encourage bushiness. Aluminum Plants wilt quickly if not given sufficient moisture.

Pilea involucrata, South American Friendship Plant, Panimiga

The oval leaves of this species are a rich coppery green, deeply quilted, and closely set on short stems at whose tips tight clusters of minute rosy flowers are borne. This dwarf type is easy to grow and very appealing as a house plant.

Pilea microphylla, Artillery Plant

The common name of this Pilea is Artillery Plant because when its miniscule blossoms are mature, they forcibly send out tiny puffs of pollen. The plants have tiny pale green leaves and stems so closely branched in flat sprays that they could easily be mistaken as Ferns. They like a partly shaded, warm site and high humidity.

Pilea numulariifolia, Creeping Charlie

This South American creeping plant has small, round, closely set, hairy leaves. It does well in a humid atmosphere as either a hanging plant or as a ground cover.

Pilea Silver Tree

This Caribbean species has much of the upright growth of the Aluminum Plant, as well as the bronzy coloring of Panimiga, but the leaves have a broad central stripe of silver, as well as silvery dots among the bronzy portions of the leaves.

Pisonia grandis tricolor, see *Heimerliodendron brunonianum variegatum*

Plectranthus, Swedish Ivy

It is difficult to determine the origin of the name Swedish Ivy, since all *Plectranthus* species are native to Australia or

Africa. At any rate, the genus includes several fine house plants, mostly suited to hanging baskets. They will grow well in a moist soil composed of equal parts of peat moss, loam, and sand and will stand quite dim light and still do well. Occasionally plants will send out terminal spikes of tiny white, pink, or lavender flowers. Swedish Ivies grow easily and rapidly, thus should not be fed more often than every three to four months.

Plectranthus australis has nearly round, clear green leaves, evenly scalloped around their edges. This is the most common species.

Plectranthus coleoides marginatus is a bushy, rather than a trailing, plant and, as its name suggests, has white-margined leaves shaped like those of its cousin, Coleus.

Plectranthus oertendahlii has fresh green leaves nicely marked with silvery veins, and its type *variegata* has foliage broadly blotched with white against a green background.

Plectranthus purpuratus has leaves of the orbicular, scalloped shape one might expect, but they are covered with a fuzz of tiny velvety hairs and are purplish on their undersides.

Polyscias (*Aralia*), Aralia

The botanical name *Aralia* was used for many years to include, not only the plants now known as *Polyscias,* but *Panax* and *Nothopanax* as well. Now all come under the one heading of *Polyscias,* with Aralia as a common name. It is no wonder that they were listed in various ways when one sees the variety of foliage displayed by members of this family. All are reasonably good house plants, although they do best when they can have more humidity than many of our homes provide. By nature, most of them are native to islands of the South Pacific, where the air is humid at all times. For that reason we find that they do especially well in coastal areas, and many are grown as outdoor plants in mild climates such as Florida and the Gulf Coast.

All tropical Aralias do well in full sun or light shade, except *P. guilfoylei victoriae,* which demands protection from sun during the brightest part of the day. Aralias are really shrubs rather than herbaceous plants and increase in height on woody stems as rather slender, narrow-growing specimens. They enjoy an evenly moist soil composed of equal parts of peat moss and sandy loam. Feeding with a mild house plant fertilizer should be confined to two or three times a year unless rapid growth is desired.

Polyscias balfouriana (Aralia balfouriana)

This species and its variety *marginata* are native to New Caledonia. Their compound leaves consist of three round coarsely toothed leaflets, which are shiny, leathery and dark green on the species and edged with white on *marginata.*

Polyscias filicifolia (Aralia filicifolia)

The specific name of this species means that it has leaves that are fernlike in appearance, which is an apt description.

Polyscias fruticosa (Aralia fruticosa)

Commercial growers sometimes refer to this species as "Parsley" because of the shape of its leaves.

Polyscias guilfoylei victoriae (Aralia guilfoylei victoriae)

The pinnate leaves of this variety are finely cut and edged in white.

Polyscias paniculata

The island of Mauritius, which lies in the Indian Ocean east of Malagasy, is the home of this species and its selected type *variegata,* which is the one most often seen in commerce. Its hard shiny leaves consist of seven leaflets, each of which is liberally blotched with creamy-white areas set on an olive-green background.

Rhoeo spathacea (*R. discolor*), Moses-in-the-cradle

Moses-in-the-cradle does not come from the banks of the Nile, as one might suspect, but from Mexico. It is a Spiderwort relative and has small white flowers (Moses) set deeply between boat-shaped bracts (the cradle) at the base of each leaf. The stiff, sword-shaped leaves themselves are the showy portions of the plant, being rich and vibrant green above, but shiny purple beneath. The variety *vittata* has leaves that are striped yellow. Give Moses-in-the-cradle bright light or filtered shade and see that the soil beneath it is evenly moist at all times. A mixture of equal parts of peat moss, loam, and sand will take care of this plant nicely, and mild feedings can be given three or four times a year. It is a good idea to divide and repot old plants so as to get more thrifty growth.

Ruellia, Ruellia

The soft green, velvety leaves of *Ruellia portellae*, which are reddish purple beneath, make this spreading plant from Brazil a natural one for hanging baskets in areas where warmth and high humidity can be maintained. This situation does not usually exist in homes, however; so Ruellias are not easy to grow as house plants. When they are happy, however, they send out a continuous display of small rosy-lavender flowers which adds to their attractiveness. They need bright light, but protection from full sun, and an evenly moist soil composed of equal parts of leaf mold, peat moss, loam, and sand. *Ruellia makoyana* is very similar to the above species, but has larger, bright carmine flowers.

Sanchezia, Sanchezia

The tropical South American country of Ecuador is home to the colorful shrub we know as *Sanchezia nobilis glaucophylla*. It is related to and has much the same appearance as *Aphelandra*, but is taller growing, becoming as much as five feet in height. Its large glossy green leaves are heavily marked along the veins with bright yellow, and its flowers, borne in heavy spikes, are yellow also. Sanchezias need a very moist, humusy soil and shelter from the sun. Small plants do well in flowerpots, but as they become larger they should be moved into tubs.

Sansevieria, Sansevieria, Bowstring Hemp, Snake Plant

The indoor gardener who is not acquainted with Sansevierias must truly be a beginner, for these ubiquitous plants have been in cultivation for many years. It should be pointed out that in addition to the common upright-growing Sansevierias, whose slender banded or striped leaves grow one and one half to two feet tall, there are the varieties whose leaves are arranged in ground-hugging rosettes. The three most common of these low growers are Hahnii, Golden Hahnii, and Silver Hahnii. The original plant appeared as a mutation in New Orleans several years ago, and subsequent sports have produced the "Gold" and "Silver" varieties.

Most of the commonly grown upright forms of Sansevierias are selections of S. *trifasciata,* as are the mutant forms described above. Sometimes this species is known as S. *zeylanica* in commerce, but the true S. *zeylanica* is a type from Ceylon rarely grown in this country. Nearly all of our Sansevierias are native to Africa, where they are said to be a favorite food for elephants.

It would be difficult to find more undemanding plants than Sansevierias. They will grow in full sunshine or very deep shadows. Nearly any soil will satisfy them, although they grow fastest in one that is half peat moss. If the soil is kept moist, they will make rapid growth, but if it is kept nearly dry, they will still remain attractive, but hardly change in size.

One feature seldom seen on young Sansevierias is blossoms, but older plants often send out slender stems set with clusters of tiny, fragrant, pinkish-white flowers.

Saxifraga sarmentosa, Strawberry-Geranium, Strawberry-Begonia

The Chinese perennial which masquerades under such names as Strawberry-Geranium and Strawberry-Begonia has no relationship to any of the plants mentioned. No doubt it received the "Strawberry" part of its common name because it sends out slender runners from a clump of basal leaves and in time will build up a colony of youngsters around the parent plant. The soft, round, hairy leaves of the species S. *sarmentosa* are purplish beneath, which adds to the attractiveness of this neat little plant which rarely grows more than three or four inches tall. Occasionally it sends up tiny spikes of misty white flowers, but its real value lies in its lovely foliage. There is a variant known as *tricolor,* which is more dwarf. Its leaves are often edged in pink and the underleaf color is more pronounced. Give these plants a regular potting soil of equal parts of peat moss, loam, and sand and let them become moderately dry between waterings. They do best in light shade but can stand sun for part of each day. In addition to their usual use as pot plants, they make unusually attractive hanging basket subjects.

Setcreasea purpurea, Purple Heart

This little Mexican plant, whose habit of growth and flowers shows its kinship to Wandering Jew, is different in that its hairy leaves are of a deep purple hue. A soil mixture of equal parts of loam, sand, and peat moss will suit this plant. This soil should be well watered, then allowed to become nearly dry before adding more moisture. Purple Heart will grow in light shade or full sun, but its full coloring will not be apparent unless given a sunny location.

Setcreasea striata, see *Callisia elegans*

Strelitzia reginae, Bird-of-Paradise

Surely every flower lover is acquainted with the exotic flowers of the Bird-of-Paradise, which combine brilliant hues of red, orange, and blue. It is not the kind of a plant for the average home because it requires an enormous amount of room in full sun in order to do well. The paddle-shaped blue-green leaves often become three to four feet tall and, since they last for years, must be kept unblemished if a specimen plant is to be ornamental. It is well suited to tub culture, where it can be given enough space to develop properly. The Bird-of-Paradise does well in an ordinary soil mixture of equal parts of peat moss, sand, and loam, which ought to be allowed to dry considerably between generous waterings. Since only large plants are apt to flower freely, feed young plants once a month with any house plant fertilizer. The Bird-of-Paradise is native to South Africa.

Tetrapanax papyriferus (Aralia papyrifera, Fatsia papyrifera), Rice Paper Plant

In Formosa, where the Rice Paper Plant is native, it lives up to its name, for paper is actually made of the pith of the stems. In mild climates it is grown as a bold garden shrub because its huge palmately lobed leaves have such an exotic aspect. No doubt it will become more commonly available from greenhouse sources as a demand increases for unusual foliage plants of heroic proportions. Give the Rice Paper Plant full sun and a moist soil composed of equal parts of loam, sand, and peat moss.

Tolmiea menziesii, Pick-a-back Plant, Youth and Old Age

The curious way in which this plant produces plantlets at the bases of its mature leaves assures it of a lasting place among medium-sized house plants. It is native to the moist western coast of North America from Alaska to northern California, where it thrives in the cool, moist shade of tall trees. In the home it continues to like similar conditions and is a wonderful plant for locations which are apt to be on the chilly side. Well-grown plants are truly beautiful, since the long leaf petioles which extend beyond the pot are weighted down in a graceful manner by their burdens of leaves and young plants. Occasionally plants will send up slender airy spikes of small white flowers. Give them a moist, highly organic soil.

Tradescantia, Wandering Jew (see also *Zebrina*)

The Wandering Jew most often seen is the species *Tradescantia fluminensis variegata,* a creeping South American plant grown for its attractive green-and-white-striped leaves. This is a very old and common house plant that does best under light shade. It should be given a humusy soil which should be allowed to become moderately dry between waterings.

Zebrina, Wandering Jew (see also *Tradescantia*)

Several forms of *Zebrina pendula,* a creeping Mexican plant, are commonly called Wandering Jew. They have rather thick-jointed, trailing stems and glistening foliage variously striped with silver, pink, and white on the upper surfaces, while the lower ones are tinged reddish purple. They like a moist, humusy soil and protection from the sun. This type of Wandering Jew prefers higher humidity than *Tradescantia,* listed above.

CHAPTER 24

CACTI AND OTHER SUCCULENT PLANTS

It is well known to most flower lovers that Cacti, as well as many other succulent plants, have some of the most beautiful flowers in the plant kingdom. For this reason, in this book devoted to foliage plants, scarce attention would be shown to them except for the fact that, in addition to their flowers, their growth habits surely include some of the most bizarre in the world. It is this side of succulent plants which qualifies them for inclusion in this text. They are plants that admirably fulfill the need for living verdure in situations which are so hot, dry, and sunny as to be unfavorable for the culture of more conventional vegetation.

Most succulent plants are native to desert regions where a hostile climate has, through the ages, forced them to find methods of conserving scanty rainfall. In most cases leaves have been dispensed with entirely, and the stems have retained chlorophyll to do the work of leaves. Rarely are desert plants injured by exposure to the full fury of the sun. They are invariably covered with a waxy layer to prevent moisture loss, or with dense hairs, spines, or scales to lessen evaporation through shading of the stems. Water conservation is further enhanced by the paucity of breathing pores on desert plants. In addition, some of them have accordionlike stems that expand or contract, depending upon moisture supplies. In these ways they have learned to live for months, and in some cases for years, without regular rainfall.

It should be pointed out that all Cacti and succulents are not desert plants. Such genera as *Schlumbergera* and *Zygocactus*, which we call Christmas Cacti, and *Epiphyllum*, the Orchid Cactus, are native to jungle regions. As such, they cannot grow with the desert succulents and, since they are grown for their flowers rather than for foliage, are not included in this book.

As house plants, Cacti and other dry-area succulents face three major conditions which are unnatural. The greatest of these is moisture, for most flower lovers feel heartless if they withhold water from them for weeks on end. Yet, this is what many Cacti must have if they are to survive as house plants. Overwatering is by far the greatest peril they must endure; thus Cacti and other succulents will often do reasonably well for neglectful gardeners who forget to water plants regularly! As a matter of fact, these plants will exist on a bare minimum of care, and, although they do not look their best, they will cling tenaciously to life.

The second danger succulent plants face is that of low levels of light. Nature has endowed them with protective devices that shield them from the sun, but they must, nonetheless, have bright sun in order to grow normally. Lack of light not only reduces the possibility of flowers to nearly zero, but it causes the plant bodies to elongate unnaturally while reaching toward whatever source of light is available. Thus, even if these plants are to be considered only from the point of view of their decorative shapes and unusual growth habits, they must have full sun in order for these features to be preserved.

It is not commonly understood that many of the succulents, especially Cacti, must have not only dry but cool conditions during their winter dormancy prior to spring flowering. In a real sense this is a factor that we cannot provide in our homes. Thus we must be more or less resigned to the fact that the plants will not be apt to blossom in our homes. This does not mean that we should not grow them, however, for the outlandish way in which many of them grow is of far greater over-all value than the lovely though fleeting beauty of their flowers.

The extraordinary variety of succulents staggers the imagination. Every continent, for example, has wide areas of desert, and in each instance certain forms of plants have become adapted to the inhospitable face of nature. A great many of the plants which we cultivate in an ordinary fashion have related species which live in deserts in other parts of the world. A plant as commonplace as our dooryard Geranium has succulent relatives living in the deserts of southwestern Africa. Many of them have thick, juicy stems and lose their leaves during part of each year; some even have thorny stubs along their branches in a manner most inconsistent with our general conception of Geraniums. Our Poinsettias, native to Mexico, have cousins in Africa and India that look like Cacti. Some are enormous, spiny plants whose only apparent link with Poinsettias is the make-up of their floral parts and the milky sap common to all. North and South America are the original homes of all true Cacti, but they have been transported by man throughout the world and in some places are so happy as to seem to be native to other lands.

The need for a sunny site has been adequately discussed, but of equal importance is a proper soil mixture that is extremely well drained so that there is never a possibility of water standing around the roots of the plants. Growers use many ingredients to suit their succulents, but the following will serve as a guide: two parts loam, one part each of coarse sand and leaf mold, plus one-half part crushed charcoal. To this add a dusting of both ground limestone and bone meal. In repotting Cacti, prevent injury to yourself by using tongs or a rolled newspaper to hold the plants.

To re-emphasize the critical matter of watering, use the following schedule as a guide: During January and February give your Cacti practically no water, except to keep plants from shriveling. In early March begin very light waterings, but by late March and during the month of April supply water liberally, for this is the period of growth. For the balance of the late spring and summer, plants do best if they can be placed outdoors where they will receive considerably less water than they had during the spring. From September until the end of the year give them only enough water to prevent dehydration.

The following Cacti should be given full sun. Some of the species are tiny plants, even when mature. Others grow to considerable size and can be used as young plants while small, or as larger specimens if they are required: *Aporocactus, Ariocarpus, Astrophytum, Cephalocereus, Cereus, Chamaecereus, Cleistocactus, Echinocactus, Echinocereus, Echinopsis, Gymnocalycium, Hylocereus, Lemaireocereus, Lobivia, Mammillaria, Melocactus, Notocactus, Nyctocereus, Opuntia, Pachycereus, Parodia, Rebutia,* and *Trichocereus.*

Other succulent plants, not Cacti, which need full sun are as follows: *Aeonium, Agave, Aloe, Bryophyllum, Caralluma, Cissus quadrangularis,* * *Cotyledon, Crassula,* ** *Echeveria, Euphorbia, Faucaria, Fenestraria, Kalanchoe,* ** *Kleinia, Lithops, Mesembryanthemum, Pachyphytum, Pedilanthus,* ** *Pleiospilos, Sedum, Sempervivum,* and *Stapelia.*

* See Chapter 21.
** See Chapter 23.

CHAPTER 25

A GARDEN IN A DISH

The charm of dish gardens (Plate 32.) remains undiminished through the years. Although they bear but little outward resemblance to the bonsai trees of Japanese horticultural art, they nonetheless communicate the same message. One should not look upon them as a collection of small plants, but as a landscape in miniature which recalls other, larger scenes of natural beauty. For that reason, dish gardens are wonderful gifts for persons who are confined to a home or hospital. In a real sense they bring outdoor gardens indoors.

A well-made dish garden consists of a collection of compatible plants growing together in a small container. The assortments may range all the way from groups of Cacti or other succulents which like a dry soil to tropical specimens which enjoy constant moisture. As long as plants which require similar conditions are planted together and given proper care, they will prosper.

One of the goals of dish garden culture is to maintain each of the plants in an attractive proportion to its neighbors. This means that plant food should be given very sparingly so as not to encourage excessive growth. The facts that the plants are set closely and that there is but little soil available help to restrain their growth. It is perfectly logical, too, to prune plants which become too large.

Most dish gardens, with the exception of those composed of succulents, should not have full sun, but instead should be given an abundance of indirect light or supplementary artificial illumination. To maintain even growth, dish gardens should be turned occasionally so all plants will receive an equal share of light.

It is easy to overwater a dish garden, since most containers have no provision for drainage. The aim, except for gardens of succulents which must be quite dry, should be to maintain the soil barely damp. Test it with your finger tips. One of the best ways to water a dish garden is to submerge the container in warm water in your kitchen sink. When bubbles cease to rise, remove it from the water and gently lay it on its side for twenty minutes to let excess moisture drain away. Usually this operation should take place at weekly intervals. It provides an opportunity to wash dust off the foliage as well as give the plants a drink.

Finally, when the day comes that a dish garden has outgrown its container, many of the plants may be potted singly and grown as house plants.

CHAPTER 26

TERRARIUMS AND INDOOR GREENHOUSES

Some things are so old that when they are rediscovered they seem to be new again. The present interest in terrariums and indoor greenhouses goes back through generations of flower lovers. Over a century ago, for example, nearly every gardener knew about Wardian Cases, named for their inventor, N. B. Ward of London. It was in 1842 that he published his treatise *Plant Growing in Closely Glazed Cases*. These were the glass-walled and glass-topped boxes used by plant hunters then, and to some extent today, to ensure the safe arrival of delicate specimens sent on long sea voyages.

Today our house plants do not have to be protected from the high winds and salt spray of an ocean passage, but they do have to contend with the insidious peril of aridity, which is a side effect of the warmth we demand in our centrally heated homes. There is no doubt but that low humidity and low levels of light are two of the most limiting factors in house plant growth. Both can be overcome by the use of what we nowadays call indoor greenhouses or terrariums.

Many of the plants included in this book have notations to the effect that they do better under the humid conditions of terrariums than they do as ordinary household plants. Some of the small Ferns such as *Pteris* and *Adiantum,* as well as *Episcia, Fittonia,* and *Maranta,* all do especially well in terrariums. Many persons who live in arid regions find that the only successful way in which they can grow African Violets is in terrariums where high levels of humidity can be maintained.

A terrarium can be in the form of a bottle, a discarded aquarium, or any glass container. It should have a glass or clear plastic cover which can be removed or raised to allow excess humidity to escape. It should never be put in a sunny place or the heat will become so intense as to parboil the plants within it. A well-lighted spot is essential, however, unless supplementary light is given.

The subject of supplementary light brings up the fact that in recent years some of the major electrical companies have put on the market special lamps which emit light rays that are especially conducive to plant growth. These will fit into ordinary fluorescent fixtures and may be mounted over a terrarium to provide extra light. Under these conditions a terrarium can be set anywhere, even in the darkest corner, and still grow beautifully.

Garden magazines carry advertisements of several styles of indoor greenhouses, but this could just as well be an intriguing do-it-yourself project for winter evenings. Let the size suit your needs. Make the frame of wood or aluminum and glaze it with glass or clear plastic. Glass is easier to clean, doesn't scratch as easily, provides better visibility, lasts longer, and adds rigidity to the structure; plastic film is less expensive initially but is short lived. Make the case self-contained with a moistureproof bottom tray to protect floors or tables and ensure portability. Do not forget to install lights for extra illumination during dark days.

Soil and soil moisture are two related subjects in terrarium culture. A mixture of equal parts of loam, sand, and peat moss will suffice for the soil, but one must be very careful not to overwater. The atmosphere in the closed terrarium is apt to be very humid, a condition the plants enjoy, but since the moisture does not evaporate easily, it is usually not necessary to water plants more than once a month. Use your own discretion and water more frequently if the soil becomes dry, but remember that under some conditions terrariums can stay closed without watering for many months, or even years. In order to keep glass clear of condensation and to admit fresh air, it is well to open the covers of terrariums occasionally.

A last word of caution might be in order. Be careful to use soil that you have reason to believe is disease free, because fungus organisms can spread quickly in the moist air of a terrarium. It may be advisable to sterilize the soil before using, but there is always the possibility of infection from a plant which has been growing in nonsterilized soil. Small quantities of soil can be easily sterilized in your oven by maintaining a temperature of 180 degrees Fahrenheit for thirty minutes. Weed seeds, as well as disease organisms, will be killed.

The need for fertilizer is very low in a terrarium because the object is to maintain plants in small sizes so as to retain correct proportions. Feed very sparingly, if at all.

SMALL PLANTS ESPECIALLY SUITED TO TERRARIUM CULTURE

Anthurium scherzerianum   *Maranta*
Chamaeranthemum   *Pellionia*
Dichorisandra   *Pilea*
Episcia   *Ruellia*
Fittonia   *Saintpaulia*
Hemigraphis

SMALL FERNS FOR TERRARIUMS

Adiantum (small varieties)
Asplenium
Cyrtomium
Davallia
Polystichum
Pteris (particularly good for small terrariums)

CHAPTER 27

LISTS OF FOLIAGE PLANTS GROUPED ACCORDING TO CULTURAL NEEDS

(SEE ALSO CHAPTERS 21, 22, 24, AND 26)

It is generally helpful to be able to find in the form of a list the various plants which may be grown under similar conditions. In the groupings below you will notice that some names appear in more than one list. This is an indication of the wide range of tolerance within these particular plants. As an additional aid, the plant lists are subdivided into categories so that one may easily find a particular type of plant that is suited to a given location: For example, *Ferns for light shade* or *Foliage plants that will grow in water*. All plants are listed by their scientific names as an aid in locating more information about them in the text or index.

PLANTS WHICH WILL GROW IN BRIGHT SUN

Aeonium	*Bryophyllum*
Agave	*Caladium*
Aloe	*Caralluma*
Ananas	*Cephalocereus*
Aporocactus	*Cereus*
Araucaria	*Chamaecereus*
Ariocarpus	*Chamaerops humilis*
Astrophytum	*Citrus*
Beaucarnea	*Cleistocactus*
Billbergia	*Codiaeum*
Bowiea	*Coleus*

PLANTS WHICH WILL GROW IN BRIGHT SUN (continued)

Cotyledon
Crassula
Echeveria
Echinocactus
Echinocereus
Echinopsis
Euphorbia
Fatshedera
Faucaria
Fenestraria
Ficus (some)
Grevillea
Gymnocalycium
Gynura
Hedera
Hibiscus
Homalocladium
Hoya
Hylocereus
Kalanchoe
Kleinia
Lemaireocereus
Lithops
Lobivia
Mammillaria
Melocactus

Mesembryanthemum
Notocactus
Nyctocereus
Opuntia
Pachycereus
Pachyphytum
Pandanus
Parodia
Phormium
Pittosporum
Pleiospilos
Podocarpus
Polyscias
Rebutia
Rhoeo
Sansevieria
Schefflera
Sedum
Sempervivum
Setcreasea
Stapelia
Strelitzia
Tetrapanax
Trichocereus
Vinca

Bromeliads for sunny places

Ananas

Billbergia

Cacti and succulents for sunny places

Aeonium
Agave
Aloe

Aporocactus
Ariocarpus
Astrophytum

Cacti and succulents for sunny places (continued)

Bryophyllum	Lemaireocereus
Caralluma	Lithops
Cephalocereus	Lobivia
Cereus	Mammillaria
Chamaecereus	Melocactus
Cleistocactus	Mesembryanthemum
Cotyledon	Notocactus
Crassula	Nyctocereus
Echeveria	Opuntia
Echinocactus	Pachycereus
Echinocereus	Pachyphytum
Echinopsis	Parodia
Euphorbia	Pleiospilos
Faucaria	Rebutia
Fenestraria	Sedum
Gymnocalycium	Sempervivum
Hylocereus	Stapelia
Kalanchoe	Trichocereus
Kleinia	

Palm for sunny places

Chamaerops humilis

PLANTS WHICH WILL GROW UNDER LIGHT SHADE

Acanthus	Asplenium
Adiantum	Begonia
Aechmea	Billbergia
Aglaonema	Bowiea
Anthurium	Buxus
Aphelandra	Caladium
Araucaria	Calathea
Asparagus	Callisia
Aspidistra	Caryota

Ceropegia
Chamaedorea
Chamaeranthemum
Chamaerops
Chlorophytum
Chrysalidocarpus
Cibotium
Cissus
Citrus
Codiaeum
Coffea
Coleus
Costus
Cordyline
Crassula
Cryptanthus
Cyathea
Cyrtomium
Davallia
Dichorisandra
Dieffenbachia
Dizygotheca
Dracaena
Dyckia
Epiphyllum
Episcia
Euonymous
Fatshedera
Fatsia
Ficus
Fittonia
Geogenanthus
Hedera
Heimerliodendron
Hemigraphis

Homalomena
Howea
Hoya
Hypoestes
Livistona
Maranta
Monstera
Neoregelia
Nephrolepis
Nephthytis
Nidularium
Pandanus
Pedilanthus
Pellionia
Peperomia
Philodendron
Phoenix
Pilea
Piper
Pittosporum
Platycerium
Plectranthus
Podocarpus
Polypodium
Polyscias
Polystichum
Pteris
Rhapsis
Rhoeo
Ruellia
Sanchezia
Sansevieria
Saxifraga
Schefflera
Schlumbergera

PLANTS WHICH WILL GROW UNDER LIGHT SHADE (continued)

Scindapsus
Senecio mikanioides
Setcreasea
Spathiphyllum
Syagrus
Syngonium
Tillandsia

Tolmiea
Trachycarpus
Tradescantia
Vinca
Vriesia
Zebrina
Zygocactus

Bromeliads for light shade

Aechmea
Billbergia
Cryptanthus
Dyckia

Neoregelia
Nidularium
Tillandsia
Vriesia

Cacti and succulents for light shade

Crassula
Epiphyllum

Schlumbergera
Zygocactus

Ferns for light shade

Adiantum
Asplenium
Cibotium
Cyathea
Cyrtomium
Davallia

Nephrolepis
Platycerium
Polypodium
Polystichum
Pteris

Palms for light shade

Caryota
Chamaedorea
Chamaerops
Chrysalidocarpus
Howea

Livistona
Phoenix
Rhapsis
Syagrus
Trachycarpus

PLANTS WHICH WILL TOLERATE DEEP SHADE

Deep shade offers the greatest challenge to growing plants, and the types which will thrive under such conditions are very limited. The following plants are those which will retain their inherent beauty longest under these trying circumstances.

Aglaonema	*Hemigraphis*
Aspidistra	*Nephthytis*
Asplenium	*Polypodium*
Chamaedorea	*Polystichum*
Cyrtomium	*Pteris*
Davallia	*Sansevieria*
Ficus pumila	*Spathiphyllum*

Ferns for deep shade

Asplenium nidus	*Polypodium*
Cyrtomium	*Polystichum*
Davallia	*Pteris*

Palm for deep shade

Chamaedorea

PLANTS WHICH SHOULD BE GIVEN DRY SOIL

Plants needing dry soil are defined as those which must have soil "on the dry side" all through the year, or which have seasonal requirements for dry soil. Check text for exact recommendations for particular plants.

Aeonium	*Aloe*
Agave	*Aporocactus*

PLANTS WHICH SHOULD BE GIVEN DRY SOIL (continued)

Ariocarpus	*Kleinia*
Astrophytum	*Lemaireocereus*
Beaucarnea	*Lithops*
Bowiea	*Lobivia*
Caralluma	*Mammillaria*
Cephalocereus	*Melocactus*
Cereus	*Mesembryanthemum*
Ceropegia	*Notocactus*
Chamaecereus	*Nyctocereus*
Cissus quadrangularis	*Opuntia*
Cleistocactus	*Pachycereus*
Cotyledon	*Pachyphytum*
Crassula	*Parodia*
Echeveria	*Peperomia*
Echinocactus	*Pleiospilos*
Echinocereus	*Rebutia*
Echinopsis	*Saxifraga*
Euphorbia	*Scindapsus*
Faucaria	*Sedum*
Fenestraria	*Sempervivum*
Grevillea	*Setcreasea*
Gymnocalycium	*Stapelia*
Hoya	*Tradescantia*
Hylocereus	*Trichocereus*
Kalanchoe	

PLANTS WHICH SHOULD BE GIVEN A SOIL
WHICH IS BARELY MOIST

Plants which need barely moist soil are defined as those which should be watered regularly enough so that the soil is never really dry and never saturated.

Acanthus	*Aglaonema*
Aechmea	*Ananas*

PLANTS WHICH SHOULD BE GIVEN A SOIL
WHICH IS BARELY MOIST (continued)

Araucaria	*Monstera*
Begonia	*Neoregelia*
Billbergia	*Nidularium*
Buxus	*Pandanus*
Cissus	*Philodendron*
Citrus	*Pittosporum*
Codiaeum	*Podocarpus*
Coffea	*Sansevieria*
Cryptanthus	*Schefflera*
Dieffenbachia	*Strelitzia*
Dyckia	*Tillandsia*
Ficus	*Vinca*
Fortunella	*Vriesia*
Hibiscus	*Zebrina*
Maranta	

PLANTS WHICH NEED A MOIST SOIL

This category is not to be construed as meaning that the plants listed will grow in a saturated soil. The fine line to be drawn is this: Keep the soil moist, but not sopping. Water should not stand around the roots at any time.

Adiantum	*Chamaerops*
Anthurium	*Chlorophytum*
Aphelandra	*Chrysalidocarpus*
Asparagus	*Cibotium*
Aspidistra	*Coleus*
Asplenium	*Cordyline*
Caladium	*Costus*
Calathea	*Cyathea*
Callisia	*Cyrtomium*
Caryota	*Davallia*
Chamaedorea	*Dichorisandra*
Chamaeranthemum	*Dizygotheca*

PLANTS WHICH NEED A MOIST SOIL (continued)

Dracaena

Episcia

Euonymous

Fatshedera

Fatsia

Fittonia

Geogenanthus

Gynura

Hedera

Heimerliodendron

Hemigraphis

Homalocladium

Homalomena

Howea

Hypoestes

Livistona

Nephrolepis

Nephthytis

Pedilanthus

Pellionia

Phoenix

Phormium

Pilea

Piper

Platycerium

Plectranthus

Polypodium

Polyscias

Polystichum

Pteris

Rhapsis

Rhoeo

Ruellia

Sanchezia

Senecio

Spathiphyllum

Syagrus

Tetrapanax

Tolmiea

Trachycarpus

FOLIAGE PLANTS WHICH WILL GROW IN WATER

It is interesting to note that several plants will grow in ordinary soil, or even dry soil, and in clear water as well, but they cannot tolerate constantly saturated, muddy soil. Many indoor gardeners have attractive vases unsuited for potted plants, but well designed for graceful water gardens. Often more than one species can be combined in foliage plant arrangements. A drop or two of a liquid plant food occasionally is sufficient for nourishment. It is considered a good idea to place some pieces of charcoal (not briquets) in the water. By doing so we find that the water does not have to be changed, but additional water has to be added to compensate for evaporation, of course.

Aglaonema
Coleus
Cordyline
Crassula argentea
Dieffenbachia
Ferns (especially Tree Fern trunks)
Hedera
Hemigraphis
Nephthytis
Philodendron, especially *cordatum* and *panduraeforme*
Scindapsus
Tradescantia
Zebrina

INDEX

(Bold-face figures indicate major references.)